NATIONAL
GEOGRAPHIC
KiDS

JUNIOR RANGER ACTIVITY BOOK

Angels Landing hiking trail winds through Zion National Park, Utah.

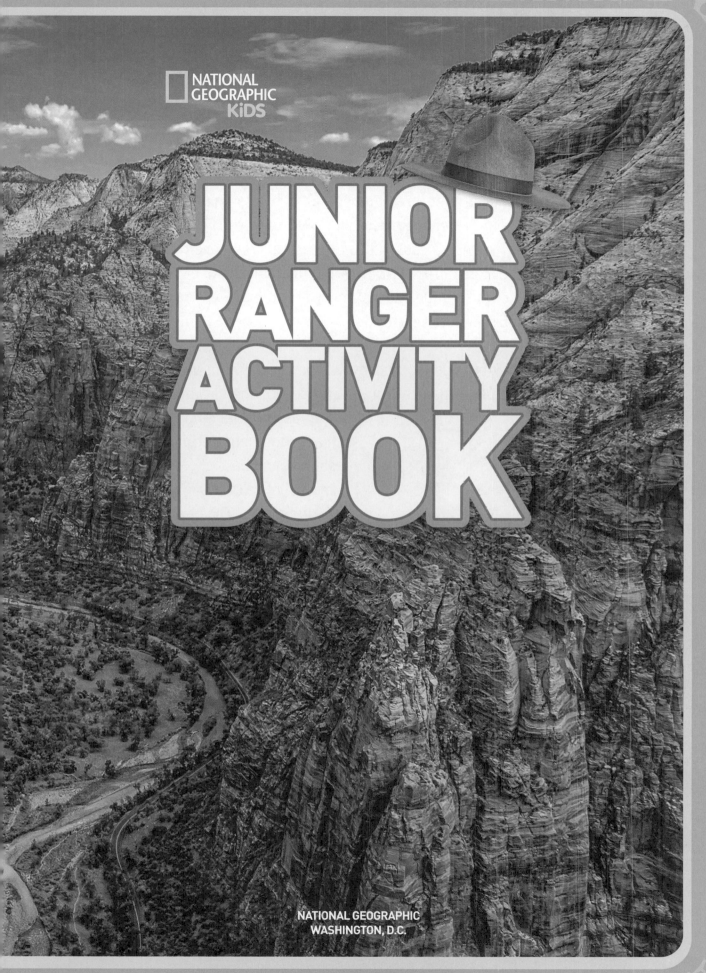

NATIONAL GEOGRAPHIC KiDS

JUNIOR RANGER ACTIVITY BOOK

NATIONAL GEOGRAPHIC
WASHINGTON, D.C.

Our Amazing National Parks

What if you could snap a photo of a wild animal, go white-water rafting, and set up a campsite all in the same day? Well, you can, in our national parks! From swamps in the Florida Everglades, to huge mesas in the Utah desert, and even the snowy wilderness of Alaska, our 59 beautiful national parks showcase all the unique ecosystems you can find within the United States and its territories.

In 1916, U.S. president Woodrow Wilson created the National Park Service, an organization that preserves the national parks, plus many more sites, such as monuments, trails, seashores, and battlefields, for a total of more than 400 unique places. The park service protects these places so that you and future generations will be able to enjoy them for years to come.

Peregrine falcon

Want to learn more about the national parks from National Geographic Kids? Visit **natgeo.com/kids/parks** for more fun!

This book will take you on an adventure through many of these national parks. Learn awesome ranger tips for the best ways to visit the parks. Plus, tiptoe around active volcanoes at Hawaiʻi Volcanoes National Park, identify the cave formations at Carlsbad Caverns, or study fossils in Badlands National Park. The possibilities are endless. Feeling inspired? What are you waiting for? Grab your backpack, binoculars, and hiking boots and hit the trails!

Become a Junior Ranger

Ever wondered what it would be like to be a national park ranger? Well, the next time you visit a park, you'll have the chance to become a Junior Ranger! All you have to do is complete an activity booklet from the visitor's center at your next park visit, give your answers to a park ranger, and receive your very own Junior Ranger patch and certificate. You'll have to answer different kinds of questions in each park, such as taking quizzes for historical sites, or learning how to think like an archaeologist in parks that have fossils, or even conducting a scavenger hunt in parks where you can spot wildlife. In order to become fully certified, all Junior Rangers must recite this oath: "Explore, Learn, and Protect!" Under this motto, you're making a promise to protect parks, learn all about the parks, and tell your family and friends how you earned your patch. Do you have what it takes to be a Junior Ranger?

Find Your Park
in the United States and Its Territories

NORTH CASCADES N.P.

OLYMPIC NATIONAL PARK

Washington

MOUNT RAINIER NATIONAL PARK

GLACIER NATIONAL PARK

CANADA
U.S.

M o n t a n a

THEODORE ROOSEVELT NATIONAL PARK

North Dakota

O r e g o n

CRATER LAKE N.P.

I d a h o

GRAND TETON NATIONAL PARK

YELLOWSTONE NATIONAL PARK

South Dakota

REDWOOD N.P.

WIND CAVE NATIONAL PARK

BADLANDS NATIONAL PARK

LASSEN VOLCANIC N.P.

W y o m i n g

PACIFIC OCEAN

California

N e v a d a

BRYCE CANYON NATIONAL PARK

Nebraska

YOSEMITE NATIONAL PARK

GREAT BASIN N.P.

U t a h

ROCKY MOUNTAIN NATIONAL PARK

KINGS CANYON N.P.

ZION NATIONAL PARK

CAPITOL REEF N.P.

ARCHES N.P.

C o l o r a d o

BLACK CANYON OF THE GUNNISON N.P.

PINNACLES N.P.

SEQUOIA N.P.

CANYONLANDS N.P.

Kansas

MESA VERDE N.P.

DEATH VALLEY N.P.

GREAT SAND DUNES N.P. & PRESERVE

CHANNEL ISLANDS N.P.

JOSHUA TREE NATIONAL PARK

GRAND CANYON NATIONAL PARK

PETRIFIED FOREST N.P.

Oklahoma

A r i z o n a

New Mexico

UNITED STATES

MEXICO

SAGUARO N.P.

CARLSBAD CAVERNS NATIONAL PARK

GUADALUPE MOUNTAINS N.P.

T e x a s

KOBUK VALLEY N.P.

GATES OF THE ARCTIC N.P. & PRESERVE

BIG BEND NATIONAL PARK

A l a s k a

DENALI NATIONAL PARK & PRESERVE

WRANGELL-ST.ELIAS N.P. & PRESERVE

LAKE CLARK N.P. & PRESERVE

GLACIER BAY N.P. & PRESERVE

KENAI FJORDS N.P.

KATMAI N.P. & PRESERVE

0   400 miles

0   400 kilometers

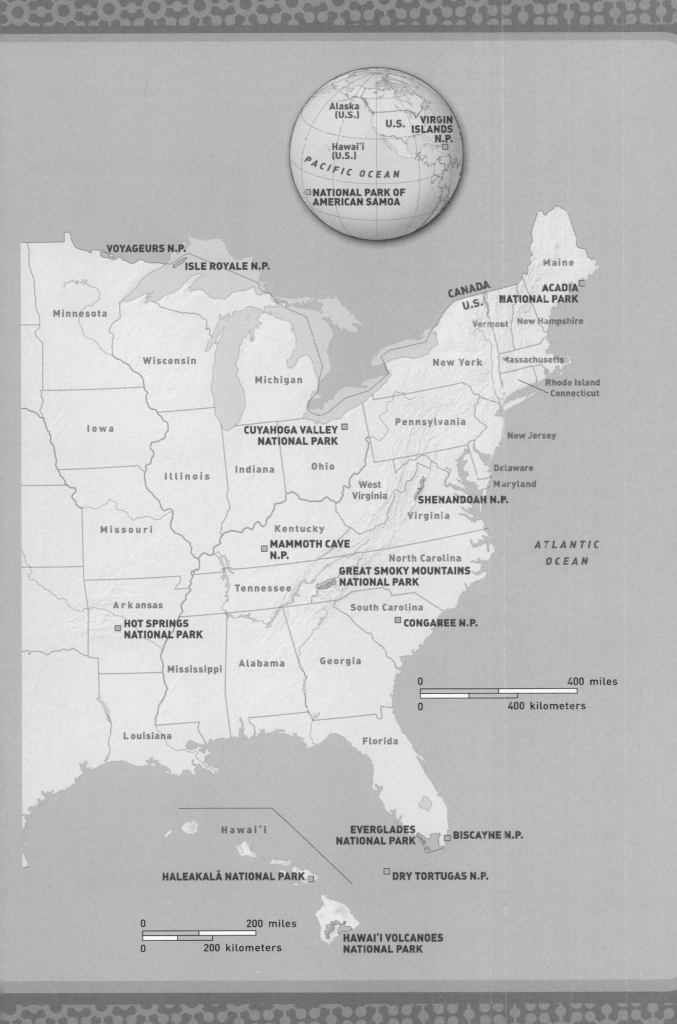

Alaska (U.S.)

U.S.

VIRGIN ISLANDS N.P.

Hawai'i (U.S.)

PACIFIC OCEAN

NATIONAL PARK OF AMERICAN SAMOA

VOYAGEURS N.P.

ISLE ROYALE N.P.

Maine

CANADA

U.S.

ACADIA NATIONAL PARK

Minnesota

Wisconsin

Vermont

New Hampshire

Michigan

New York

Massachusetts

Rhode Island

Connecticut

Iowa

CUYAHOGA VALLEY NATIONAL PARK

Pennsylvania

Illinois

Indiana

Ohio

New Jersey

Delaware

Maryland

West Virginia

SHENANDOAH N.P.

Missouri

Kentucky

Virginia

ATLANTIC OCEAN

MAMMOTH CAVE N.P.

North Carolina

GREAT SMOKY MOUNTAINS NATIONAL PARK

Tennessee

Arkansas

South Carolina

HOT SPRINGS NATIONAL PARK

CONGAREE N.P.

Mississippi

Alabama

Georgia

0 ————— 400 miles

0 ————— 400 kilometers

Louisiana

Florida

Hawai'i

EVERGLADES NATIONAL PARK

BISCAYNE N.P.

HALEAKALĀ NATIONAL PARK

DRY TORTUGAS N.P.

0 ————— 200 miles

0 ————— 200 kilometers

HAWAI'I VOLCANOES NATIONAL PARK

Games, Jokes, and More!

Pick up your pencil and get ready for tons of interactive, brainteasing fun. *Junior Ranger Activity Book* is packed with games, puzzles, and quizzes based on the national parks. The answers to activities are at the back of the book, but try to figure out the games on your own before you sneak a peek. And don't forget to share the fun with your family and friends! Check out what you'll find inside:

Fun Facts and Trivia
Learn amazing facts and figures and impress your family and friends with your knowledge of national park wildlife, history, and geography.

Funny Fill-ins
Create a wacky story starring YOU! Ask a friend to give you words to fill in the blanks without showing it to him or her. Then read it out loud for a laugh.

Jokes
Sharpen your comedy skills with these sidesplitting knock-knocks, tongue twisters, and more.

Visual Puzzles

No, your eyes are not playing tricks on you. Common objects seen from unusual angles will test your eyesight and perception.

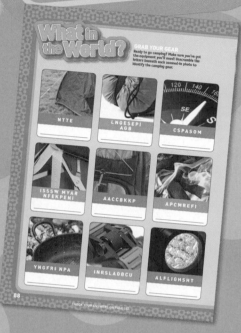

Quizzes

Test yourself and your family and friends on the wildest, wackiest, and most exciting stuff in our national parks!

Games

A selection of fun activities will test your determination, patience, and ability to spot hidden objects and creatures.

National Parks ROAD TRIP!

Great Smoky Mountains

Are you ready for exciting adventures, awesome animals, and spectacular scenery? America's national parks have all that and more. Let's warm up with some trivia questions.

1 Which national park is the most visited park in the United States?

a. Yosemite (California)
b. Yellowstone (Wyoming)
c. Grand Canyon (Arizona)
d. Great Smoky Mountains (from North Carolina to Tennessee)

Glacier Bay

2 **True or false?** Every year, about 600 humpback whales visit the seas around Glacier Bay National Park and Preserve (Alaska).

3 **True or false?** Yellowstone's famous geyser "Old Faithful" was named in 1870 after a grizzly bear that showed up every morning to shower in its waters.

Old Faithful

4 Water starting out in Glacier National Park (Montana) eventually winds up in the _____.

a. Pacific Ocean
b. Gulf of Mexico
c. Hudson Bay
d. all of the above

5 The Lakota people called this South Dakota park "land bad" long ago because there is little water and the land is rugged.

a. Badlands
b. Devils Tower
c. Wind Cave
d. Mount Rushmore

Rugged scenery of a South Dakota national park

6 There are more than 500 islands in Voyageurs National Park, in the state of _____.

a. Minnesota
b. Florida
c. Washington
d. Hawaii

Sequoia tree

7 In which California park can you find a famous tree about 2,300 years old?

a. Sequoia National Park
b. Sea World
c. Disneyland
d. Joshua Tree

8 The Kolob Arch, 287.4 feet (87.6 m) long and one of the world's largest freestanding natural arches, is in which national park?

a. Grand Canyon (Arizona)
b. Grand Teton (Wyoming)
c. Zion (Utah)
d. Yosemite (California)

9 True or false? Theodore Roosevelt National Park (North Dakota) is one of the only areas in the West where you can find herds of wild horses.

Cliff Palace

10 For more than 700 years, Pueblo Indians lived in homes built into the cliffs of what is now part of which national park?

a. Mesa Verde (Colorado)
b. Volcanoes National Park (Hawai'i)
c. Big Bend (Texas)
d. Carlsbad Caverns (New Mexico)

11 True or false? In the early 1920s, a visitor could ride into the Bat Cave at Carlsbad Caverns in a big container also used to gather bat guano (droppings).

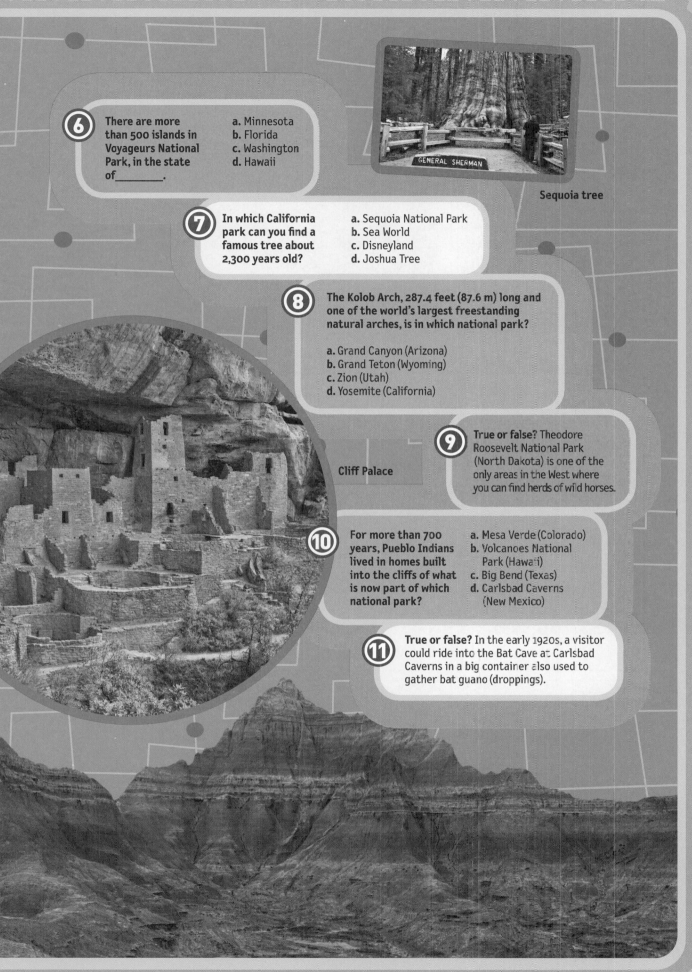

What in the World?

BEST OF THE NORTHWEST

In the Pacific Northwest states of Oregon and Washington, you may see an active volcano, a lake as deep as some skyscrapers are high, mountain glaciers, rocky beaches, historic sites, and a lot of wildlife. Unscramble the letters to identify animals, landmarks, and other national park features in these zoomed-in photos.

NIRHOGB PEEHS

_____

DEORWDO RSETE

_____

ASE TORET

_____

EDR CORK BACR

_____

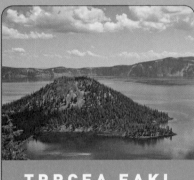

TRRCEA EAKL

_____

ELKP TFRESO

_____

AOCR

_____

UOMTN EANIRIR

_____

TORNNERH MYYPG WOL

_____

CHECK YOUR ANSWERS ON PAGE 146.

Funny Fill-In

Get ready to let off some steam in Yellowstone National Park! Established as America's very first national park, this sprawling wonderland stretches across Idaho, Montana, and Wyoming, and boasts the world's biggest collection of spouting geysers and bubbling hot springs! Plus, as home to some of our planet's coolest animals, such as wolves, bears, bison, and more, there's so much to discover!

Fun Fact! American bison weigh up to 2,000 pounds (907 kg), yet they can jump up to six feet (1.8 m) into the air!

Yellowstone National Park

We're going on a national park tour, starting in Wyoming at America's oldest national park,

Yellowstone. We _____ onto a walkway in front of the park's _____
_{verb}   adjective ending in –est

attraction: Old Faithful. The ranger tells us that the geyser got its name because it erupts

about every _____ minutes. We're getting _____ waiting for it to erupt, when
_{number}   feeling

_____ points with his/her _____ and shouts, "_____ over there!"
friend's name   body part   verb

A herd of _____ bison is _____ toward us. Some of them are as big as
large number   verb ending in –ing

a(n) _____ , with horns as long as a(n) _____ . But what really surprises us is
type of vehicle   noun

when one of them _____ into the air like _____ . _____ ,
verb ending in –s   famous basketball player   exclamation

I didn't know bison could jump! We're so busy watching the bison that we miss seeing Old

Faithful erupt. Oh well, only _____ more minutes left to wait until it happens again!
_{number}

Just Joking

KNOCK, KNOCK.

Who's there?
Owl.
Owl who?
Owl wait while you get ready.

The snowy owl is a silent hunter that can be found in woodland national parks as far south as Alabama in the winter. These owls eat their prey whole.

Q Why do skunks make **terrible** waiters?

A Because their service stinks.

You've **got** to be joking ...

Q What kind of **insect** eats **brains**?

A A zom-bee.

MALE DEER: Oh no, we'll never get home now!
FEMALE DEER: Why don't we keep going?
MALE DEER: Because the buck stops here.

Bet you didn't know

5 **crazy facts** about **creepy crawlies**

1 **Ladybugs** hibernate for up to nine months in colonies that may contain **thousands** of the spotted insects.

Insects and spiders are small but interesting national park residents. Plus, they're the most abundant creatures on Earth! So when you're visiting a park, don't forget to look down!

2 **Crickets** **create** a chirping sound by **rubbing** their front wings **together.**

3 Tiger beetles have **ears** under their **wings** and can **hear** only while **flying.**

4 Dragonflies and **damselflies** are older than **dinosaurs.**

5 Joshua Tree **National Park** in California is home to **tarantulas** as **big** as a person's hand.

With snowy slopes, gigantic glaciers, and even spectacular sled dogs, Alaska's supersized Denali National Park is crammed with cool things to see and do. Towering above all this is the massive, snow-covered peak of Denali (formerly known as Mount McKinley), a Native American word meaning "the high one" or "the great one." So bundle up and get ready to explore this amazing treeless tundra!

Fun Fact! Denali National Park's only amphibian is the tiny wood frog. It freezes solid in winter and then thaws in spring.

Denali National Park

We're heading way up north to this park and preserve in Alaska—home to North America's tallest mountain. And I want to _____ it! We join an expedition and buy supplies:
_{verb}

waterproof _____, warm _____, dehydrated _____, a
_{noun, plural}   _{clothing item, plural}   _{type of food}

gas _____, and a fleece _____. The park ranger says we'll be on the moun-
_{kitchen appliance}   _{noun}

tain for several days. That's a long time without _____. Day 1: Long climb,
_{favorite video game}

but what a(n) _____ view! Day 2: _____ up the mountain all day. Spot a golden
_{adjective}   _{verb}

eagle! Day 3: _____ around, then build a rock _____! Days 4 and 5: Trapped in
_{verb}   _{noun}

a(n) _____ by a snowstorm. Day 6: _____. Day 7: We _____ for
_{noun}   _{verb ending in –ing}   _{verb}

a(n) _____. Day 8: I miss my warm, _____ _____. Day 9: I smell
_{period of time}   _{adjective}   _{noun}

like _____. Day 10: We haven't gotten very far—I can still see where we started from!
_{type of food}

Find the HIDDEN ANIMALS

Prey animals—those that may be eaten by predators—often blend into their environment for protection. Find each animal listed below in one of the photographs. Write the letter of the correct photo next to the animal's name.

1. flounder _____
2. pika _____
3. deer _____
4. Carolina anole _____

Perfect Match

Somehow nine sets of identical twins and one set of triplets all ended up in this park at the same time. Find the look-alike(s) for each numbered park visitor. Hint: For each correct match, the clothing is identical, but some of the kids are wearing different sports gear.

The **Mount Vernon Trail** along the George Washington Memorial Parkway in **Virginia**, sees an average of **20,000 bikers**, walkers, and more every week.

GIRLS' SHOWERS

In **Congaree** National Park (South Carolina) you can **paddle down** a canoe trail to view some of North America's **tallest trees.**

Name That WILDFLOWER

Spring brings an explosion of wildflowers to many national parks, like this field of color in California's Death Valley National Park. Try to identify these bouquets of blooms from far-flung corners of the country.

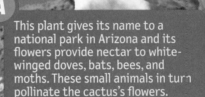

A This plant gives its name to a national park in Arizona and its flowers provide nectar to white-winged doves, bats, bees, and moths. These small animals in turn pollinate the cactus's flowers.

B In Glacier National Park in Montana, this flower sends its green shoots up through the snow in spring.

C Shenandoah National Park, Virginia, is famous for the plentiful blooms of this flower in June.

Bloom beauties

Each spring, thousands of daffodils and tulips bloom in Lady Bird Johnson Park. The park, on an island in Washington, D.C.'s Potomac River, honors the former first lady for her work to beautify America's cities and highways.

D This rare flower grows in the crater of the volcano Haleakalā, in Hawaii's Haleakalā National Park.

CHECK YOUR ANSWERS ON PAGE 146.

STUMP
YOUR PARENTS

Do your parents know their way around the national parks? If not, maybe you can help them navigate!

1 Coyotes can be spotted near the Snake River in which national park?
a. Grand Teton (Wyoming)
b. Big Bend (Texas)
c. Haleakala (Hawaii)
d. Isle Royale (Michigan)

2 The Ohio & Erie Canal Towpath Trail was used by mules and horses to pull canal boats loaded with freight along the canal in the 1800s. Now it's a place to hike, run, and bike in _____.

a. Chesapeake and Ohio Canal National Historic Park (Maryland)
b. James A. Garfield National Historic Site (Ohio)
c. Captain John Smith Chesapeake National Historic Trail (Maryland)
d. Cuyahoga Valley National Park (Ohio)

3 In which one of these national parks would you NOT find a glacier?
a. Rocky Mountain (Colorado)
b. Olympic (Washington State)
c. Petrified Forest (Arizona)
d. Great Basin (Nevada)

4 Black Canyon of the Gunnison National Park, with its steep, narrow gorge, is in which state?
a. Arizona   c. Colorado
b. New Mexico   d. Idaho

5 In Guadalupe Mountains National Park (Texas), you might see _____ .
a. hairy woodpeckers
b. coyotes
c. the highest point in Texas
d. all of the above

6 In Redwood National Park (California) you'll see the tallest type of tree in the world—the coast redwood. This tree is native to only two states: California and _____.
a. Washington   c. Idaho
b. Oregon   d. Alaska

7 Which of these national parks is home to an active volcano?
a. Great Smoky Mountains (Tennessee to North Carolina)
b. Rocky Mountain (Colorado)
c. Mount Rainier (Washington)
d. Badlands (South Dakota)

8 Which national park is NOT in Florida?
a. Everglades
b. Dry Tortugas
c. Isle Royale
d. Biscayne

9 What notable geological structure can you find in Capitol Reef National Park (Utah)?
a. Delicate Arch
b. Waterpocket Fold
c. San Andreas Fault
d. Meteor Crater

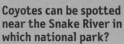

NATIONAL PARK SERVICE

CHECK YOUR ANSWERS ON PAGE 146.

What in the World?

NELDOG TGAE ERGDIB

_____

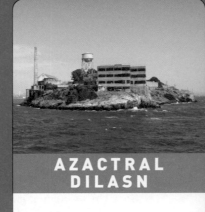

AZACTRAL DILASN

_____

ANHG REIDLG

_____

DRE-DEILAT WAHK

_____

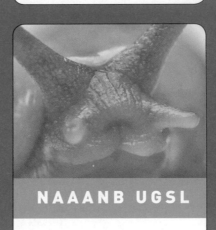

NAAANB UGSL

_____

EAS NOIL

_____

TRUSO BSHTA

_____

EPSPOPI

_____

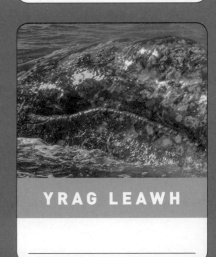

YRAG LEAWH

_____

Just Joking

The great blue heron, seen in many wetland national parks, is the largest North American heron, with a wingspan of up to 54 inches (137 cm).

KNOCK, KNOCK.

Who's there?
Raisin.
Raisin who?
Is there a raisin you aren't opening this door?

You've **got** to be joking ...

Q How do **turtles** talk to each **other?**

A On their shell phones.

Q What do you call a **frog rock star?**

A Toad-ally cool!

TONGUE TWISTER!

Say this fast three times:

Jack's knapsack strap snapped.

JIM: How do trees feel in the springtime?
NANCY: Re-leaved!

National Parks

TRIVIA CHALLENGE

If you want to feel the heat from an erupting volcano or explore a prehistoric cave, which national park would you visit? The United States is home to over 400 national park units that are visited by more than 290 million people every year. Take this trivia challenge and find out how much you know about these amazing natural treasures.

2 Which of these adventures can you have at this park—home to one of the planet's most active volcanoes?

A. walk through a lava tube
B. hike on Kilauea volcano while it's erupting
C. check out Halemaumau Crater, the legendary home of Pele the volcano goddess
D. all of the above

1 This desert destination is named after the wacky-looking twisted trees that appear throughout its 800,000 acres. Which desert could you be in if you visited this park?

A. Sahara
B. Mojave Desert
C. Kalahari Desert
D. Antarctica—the coldest desert on Earth!

JOSHUA TREE NATIONAL PARK, California

HAWAI'I VOLCANOES NATIONAL PARK, Hawaii

3 What funny name is used for the bizarre, totem pole–shaped rock formations at this destination?

A. gremlins
B. rock-and-rollers
C. chutes and ladders
D. hoodoos

BRYCE CANYON NATIONAL PARK, Utah

4 This marshy wetland is teeming with wildlife. According to legend, which of its many animals did early sailors mistake for mermaids?

A. alligator
B. Atlantic sturgeon
C. West Indian manatee
D. water snake

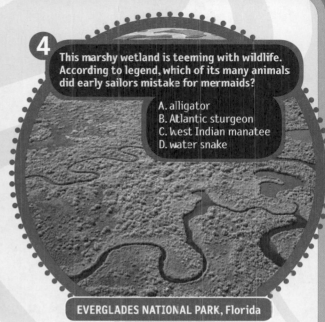

EVERGLADES NATIONAL PARK, Florida

5 If these four animals—which live in this scenic park—competed in a 50-yard (45.7-m) dash, which one would win?

A. bison
B. pronghorn
C. beaver
D. grizzly bear

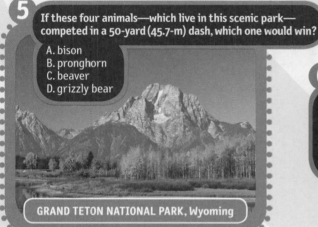

GRAND TETON NATIONAL PARK, Wyoming

6 This park is known for its scorching climate and its snow-covered mountaintops. Which of these extremes would you find here?

A. the driest spot in North America
B. the hottest spot in North America
C. the lowest spot in North America
D. all of the above

DEATH VALLEY NATIONAL PARK, California and Nevada

7 There are 116 limestone caves in this park. Which is the real explanation for how these caves were formed?

A. Humans created the caves so trains could pass through the mountains.
B. Melting glaciers wore away the rock during the last ice age.
C. Sulfuric acid dissolved the limestone over millions of years.
D. Prehistoric cavemen carved out the caves for shelter.

CARLSBAD CAVERNS NATIONAL PARK, New Mexico

8 When you strap on your snorkel mask and swim along the park's underwater snorkel trail, which of these sea creatures are you most likely to spot?

A. sea otter
B. walrus
C. sea star
D. giant squid

VIRGIN ISLANDS NATIONAL PARK, Virgin Islands

Wing-flapping BAT facts

The bats that live in Carlsbad Caverns National Park are famous, but if you keep your eyes open at dusk, you might spy these night-flying mammals at other national parks, too.

Bats are the only MAMMALS that can FLY.

A BAT CAN EAT **3,000** INSECTS IN ONE NIGHT.

SOME BATS' HEARING IS STRONG ENOUGH TO DETECT THE SOUND OF A BEETLE WALKING ON A LEAF.

Bats' knees face BACKWARD.

More than **5,000 BATS** per minute pour out of Carlsbad Cavern at peak hours in the evening.

Undersea Skiing

At Acadia, Biscayne, and Virgin Islands parks you can explore the Atlantic Ocean. Here, ocean creatures have gathered at an imaginary undersea ski lodge. Join the fun and find the 15 listed items!

1. treasure chest
2. inner tube
3. scarf
4. book
5. earmuffs
6. pail
7. sand castle
8. scuba mask
9. playing cards
10. carrot
11. cookies
12. hot cocoa
13. postcard
14. chandelier
15. sled

Swimming in the ocean at **Acadia?** Then be ready for a **chill**—the water is only **55°F** (13°C) in the **summer.**

What in the World?

PARK TRAVEL

Leave the car and check out different ways to move around parks. Unscramble the letters to identify the many wild ways to travel.

RIATOAB

EULM

KKYAA

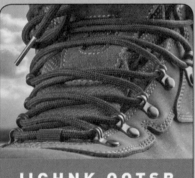

IIGHNK OOTSB

HEITW-RAWET TRAF

SSCRO-CTRYOUN KSSI

OOESNSWSH

RYFER

EASTM RATIN

CHECK YOUR ANSWERS ON PAGE 147.

Name That SHELL

Seashells are like treasures scattered on the shore, waiting to be found. When visiting a national park or seashore, see if you can name some of the shells you find.

A With a distinct five-pointed sea star shape on its back, this seashell found on Atlantic and Pacific national seashores is valuable just by its name!

B The creature that lives in this shell isn't usually aggressive but probably got its name because its strong foot enables it to hop and jump. Look for it on beaches along the southern Atlantic Ocean and the Gulf of Mexico.

C These shells are found on seashores where the ocean is warm, mostly on the southern East Coast. They were used as money for hundreds of years.

Beachcombing

There are ten national seashores and four national lakeshores for people to enjoy. Just be sure to check beach rules before collecting shells. At Padre Island National Seashore in Texas, visitors can keep up to a five-gallon (19-L) bucket filled with beachcombing treasures.

D "Mary, Mary, Quite Contrary ..." might be able to help you identify this shell. This saltwater clam washes up on many beaches, including Biscayne National Park (Florida).

A nautilus shell on a Florida beach

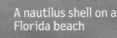

29

CHECK YOUR ANSWERS ON PAGE 147.

GRAND CANYON ADVENTURE

President Theodore Roosevelt said the Grand Canyon was "the one great sight" every American should see. Whether you take a short hike at the top, ride a mule into the chasm, or raft the river at the bottom, you're sure to see some great sights on your way.

1 The Grand Canyon is one of the top tourist destinations in the United States. About how many people visit each year?

a. 100,000   c. 1 million
b. 500,000   d. 5 million

2 **True or false?** The bottom layers of rock are the oldest, while the top layers are the youngest.

3 You can go white-water rafting down which river that flows through the Grand Canyon?

a. Rio Grande
b. Mississippi
c. Colorado
d. Missouri

4 **True or false?** No one lives in the Grand Canyon.

5 The canyon's red rocks get their color from _____, just like the soil on Mars.

a. iron
b. nickel
c. silver
d. gold

6 Which of the following is NOT one of the ways you can explore the Grand Canyon?

a. on foot   c. Jeep
b. raft   d. mule

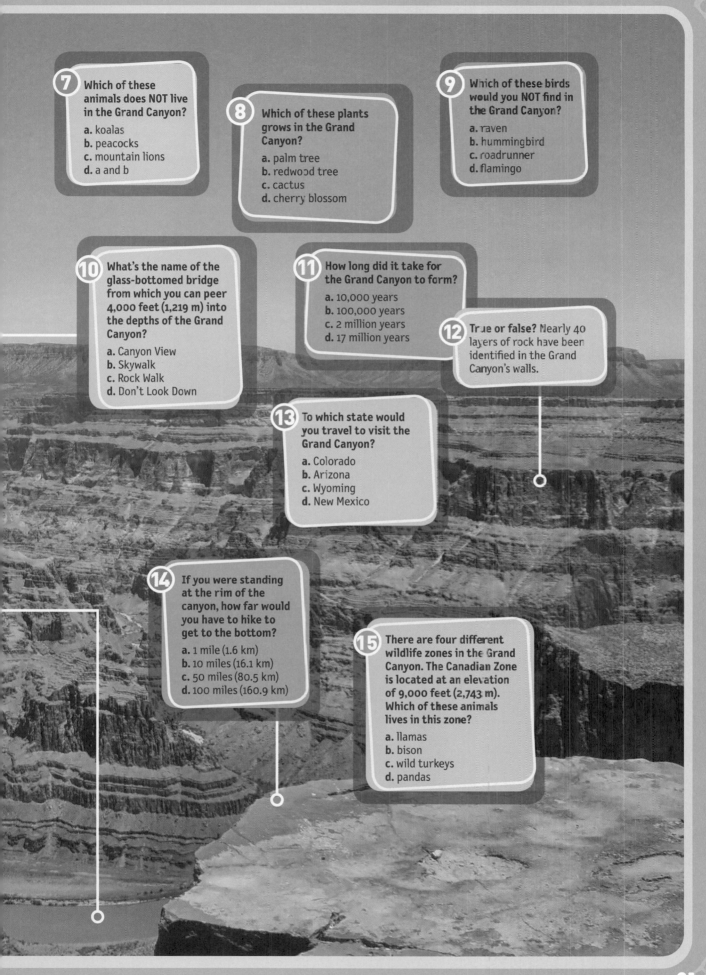

7 Which of these animals does NOT live in the Grand Canyon?

a. koalas
b. peacocks
c. mountain lions
d. a and b

8 Which of these plants grows in the Grand Canyon?

a. palm tree
b. redwood tree
c. cactus
d. cherry blossom

9 Which of these birds would you NOT find in the Grand Canyon?

a. raven
b. hummingbird
c. roadrunner
d. flamingo

10 What's the name of the glass-bottomed bridge from which you can peer 4,000 feet (1,219 m) into the depths of the Grand Canyon?

a. Canyon View
b. Skywalk
c. Rock Walk
d. Don't Look Down

11 How long did it take for the Grand Canyon to form?

a. 10,000 years
b. 100,000 years
c. 2 million years
d. 17 million years

12 True or false? Nearly 40 layers of rock have been identified in the Grand Canyon's walls.

13 To which state would you travel to visit the Grand Canyon?

a. Colorado
b. Arizona
c. Wyoming
d. New Mexico

14 If you were standing at the rim of the canyon, how far would you have to hike to get to the bottom?

a. 1 mile (1.6 km)
b. 10 miles (16.1 km)
c. 50 miles (80.5 km)
d. 100 miles (160.9 km)

15 There are four different wildlife zones in the Grand Canyon. The Canadian Zone is located at an elevation of 9,000 feet (2,743 m). Which of these animals lives in this zone?

a. llamas
b. bison
c. wild turkeys
d. pandas

6 *dino*-mite facts about dinosaurs

Do you dig dinosaurs? Visit Dinosaur National Monument in Utah! It holds one of the world's greatest collections of dinosaur fossils.

1 **T. rex** could gulp **100 pounds** (45 kg) of meat at once.

2 **Meat-eating** dinos laid **long, thin eggs;** plant-eaters laid **round** ones.

3 **Some** dinosaurs were **no bigger than chickens.**

4 No one **knows** what **color** dinosaurs were.

5 **More dinosaurs** have been found in North America than anywhere **else.**

6 Scientists once thought *Stegosaurus* had a second **brain** in its hip.

TAKE A LOOK! OLYMPIC NATIONAL PARK

TRAIL

< FIND THESE **NATIONAL PARK** ITEMS >

1 compass	2 tents	4 mountain
3 raccoons	3 deer	goats
1 bear	2 kayaks	1 marmot
3 owls	2 bald eagles	1 puma
1 slug	2 frogs	1 wolf
1 hawk		

Fun Fact!

Gray whales swim near **Olympic National Park** on their **migration** between Alaska and **Baja** California.

Double Take

See if you can spot 11 differences in the two pictures below.

National Mall, Washington, D.C.

CHECK YOUR ANSWERS ON PAGE 147.

Find the HIDDEN ANIMALS

Camouflage—coloring that blends with the environment—can help predators hide from their prey. Find the animals listed below in the photographs. Write the letter of the correct photo next to each animal's name.

1. copperhead _____
2. crocodile _____
3. coyote _____
4. screech owl _____

A

B

C

D

Just Joking

The harbor seal, found at Golden Gate National Recreation Area, can stay underwater for up to 30 minutes before it needs to come up for air.

KNOCK, KNOCK.

Who's there?
Mayan.
Mayan who?
Never mayan, I'll come back later.

Q What kind of TV shows do **fish watch?**

A Car-tunas.

TONGUE TWISTER!

Say this fast three times:

Furry felines follow fast ferrets.

MR. HEDGEHOG: Do you like my new hat?
MRS. HEDGEHOG: Lookin' sharp!

You've got to be joking ...

Q Why do eagles make great movie actors?

A Because they are very talon-ted.

Take the Plunge

Coral reef **ecosystems** are so **diverse** they are sometimes called the "rain forests of the sea."

National parks in Florida, the Virgin Islands, American Samoa, and Guam preserve coral reefs. Help this scuba diver find these items that don't belong on reefs:

1. toy car
2. in-line skate
3. wristwatch
4. peanut butter
5. beach ball
6. sneaker
7. sunglasses
8. bananas
9. suntan lotion
10. scooter
11. boat oar

CHECK YOUR ANSWERS ON PAGE 148.

Funny FiLL-IN

How does anything survive in Death Valley National Park? Located in California and Nevada, this scorching desert looks like the surface of the moon! Desert creatures have adapted to the hot conditions, but if you're going to visit and explore, make sure you pack plenty of water!

Fun Fact! "Alien," or invasive, species can be harmful to the plants and animals found in the parks naturally.

WATER

Death Valley National Park

It's so _____ that we could probably cook
      adjective

a(n) _____ on the sand! I'm so _____ I could drink _____ glasses
      type of food   adjective   large number

of _____ . We _____ over to Badwater Basin, where we see a pool of water.
    type of liquid   verb

_____ and I quickly _____ to the ground to fill our _____ .
friend's name   verb   noun, plural

"_____ !" shouts the park ranger. "Drinking that will make you feel like a(n)
    verb

_____ _____ ." So instead we head to Dante's View to watch the sun set
verb ending in –ing   noun

over the salt flats and the sand dunes. "_____ ! Are we still on Earth?" I ask when
                                          exclamation

I see the sky turn _____ and _____ above the cliffs. _____ jokes,
                    color   color   same friend's name

"My name is _____-lexor. Welcome to _____ ... " Just then we see
            silly word   name of a planet

something _____ and flash across the sky. Could it be ... ?
          verb

5 cool facts about camping

Going camping is a great way to get out and see the national parks up close. So pack a bag, set up your tent, and check out these fun facts about camping.

1 **GORP**, a nickname for **trail mix,** stands for "good old raisins and peanuts."

2 Visitors to America's **Great Smoky Mountains** National Park can enjoy more than **1,000** campsites.

3 The recipe for **s'mores,** a popular fireside snack, first appeared in a 1927 **Girl Scout** handbook.

4 Some tents are now equipped with **solar** or electrical systems to allow campers to charge their **electronic devices.**

5 In the United States alone, some **40 million** people go **camping** every year.

MAP MANIA!

PARK EXPLORER

From south to north, from east to west, which park do you like the best? Try answering these questions, then find the correct location on the map for each national park.

1 GREAT SMOKY MOUNTAINS

In this park, there are 30 or more different kinds of:

a. bears
b. salamanders
c. squirrels
d. woodpeckers

2 GRAND TETON

Which is NOT a peak in this park's Teton Range?
a. Denali (Mount McKinley)
b. Teewinot
c. Middle Teton
d. South Teton

3 ZION

More than 200 different kinds of birds fly through this park every year. Which of these does NOT?

a. canyon wren
b. wild turkey
c. blue-footed booby
d. American dipper

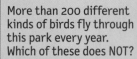

4 ACADIA

Which of these might you see in this coastal park?
a. woolly mammoth
b. redwood tree
c. lighthouse
d. glacier

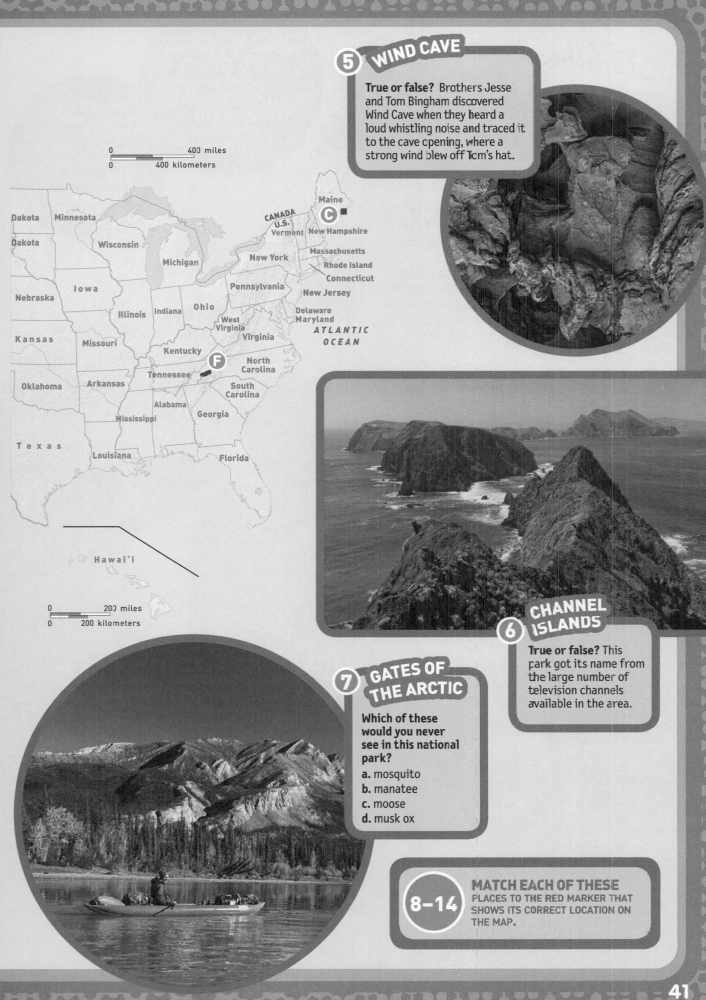

⑤ WIND CAVE

True or false? Brothers Jesse and Tom Bingham discovered Wind Cave when they heard a loud whistling noise and traced it to the cave opening, where a strong wind blew off Tom's hat.

⑥ CHANNEL ISLANDS

True or false? This park got its name from the large number of television channels available in the area.

⑦ GATES OF THE ARCTIC

Which of these would you never see in this national park?

a. mosquito
b. manatee
c. moose
d. musk ox

8–14 MATCH EACH OF THESE PLACES TO THE RED MARKER THAT SHOWS ITS CORRECT LOCATION ON THE MAP.

NATIONAL GEOGRAPHIC

ANIMAL JAM

Black Canyon of the Gunnison National Park, Colorado, **is so deep** and so narrow that **sunlight reaches the bottom** only briefly at **midday.**

Bryce Canyon National Park in Utah is filled with **hoodoos—** limestone spires **created by weather** and **erosion.**

Going on a national park camping trip? The Animal Jam characters want to camp in a canyon. Help them gather their camping gear.

1. backpack
2. compass
3. flashlight
4. map
5. sleeping bag
6. canteen
7. binoculars
8. lantern
9. walkie-talkie
10. first-aid kit
11. hiking boots
12. sunglasses
13. camera
14. climbing rope
15. skillet
16. bicycle

What in the World?

GET YOUR FEET WET

Have you ever gone tide-pooling? Look for a rocky shore, such as those in Acadia National Park. When the tide goes out, it leaves seawater trapped in small depressions in the rock. Many colorful plants and animals live in tide pools. Unscramble the letters to identify what's in these zoomed-in photos.

AES CNURHI

_____

ACBARESNL

_____

ESA ARST

_____

ASE NENAMEO

_____

EEEDSAW

_____

EHITRM RCBA

_____

MPETIL

_____

SHLYJLEFI

_____

OSBTREL

_____

43

Name That BIRD

Out in the national parks you might see some birds you recognize, and others that are new to you. How many of these do you know?

A
The males of this species make an eye-catching streak of red flying overhead. You'll see these birds in parks all across the eastern United States.

B
As its name says, it is brightly colored and has a big, strong beak. It is a visitor to parks in Florida and islands to the south.

C
These lightning-fast birds are quick to beat out the competition for nectar from their favorite flowers. As long-distance migrants, you'll see them in different seasons from California to Alaska to the Rocky Mountains.

Spot that bird

More species of birds—at least 450—can be found in Big Bend National Park, Texas, than in any other national park.

D
Often known as the "wild canary" and with a distinctive flight call, *per-chick-o-ree*, this small bird can be seen in most parks. It likes to feed on thistles and sunflowers.

44

CHECK YOUR ANSWERS ON PAGE 148.

STUMP
YOUR PARENTS

You'd probably recognize a herd of bison if you saw one in a national park. But would you and your parents know what to call these other animal groups you spot?

1 What is a group of porcupines called?
- **a.** a prickle
- **b.** a poke
- **c.** a ponder
- **d.** a party

2 A squabble is a group of _____ .
- **a.** children
- **b.** seagulls
- **c.** monkeys
- **d.** hornets

3 If you saw hundreds of grasshoppers approaching, you'd be correct if you called them _____ .
- **a.** a cloud
- **b.** a pod
- **c.** an army
- **d.** a troop

4 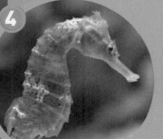 Seahorses gather in groups called_____ .
- **a.** herds
- **b.** fleets
- **c.** congresses
- **d.** teams

5 A group of_____ is known as a raft.
- **a.** lobsters
- **b.** furniture
- **c.** sea otters
- **d.** seashells

6 A group of crabs is called a _____ .
- **a.** cast
- **b.** college
- **c.** parliament
- **d.** none of the above

7 A bale is a group of_____ .
- **a.** crows
- **b.** mosquitoes
- **c.** turtles
- **d.** trucks

8 A coterie refers to a group of _____ .
- **a.** peacocks
- **b.** prairie dogs
- **c.** butterflies
- **d.** ducks

9 A group of jellyfish—a favorite meal of leatherback turtles—is called a _____ .
- **a.** flotilla
- **b.** swarm
- **c.** flock
- **d.** smack

CHECK YOUR ANSWERS ON PAGE 148.

5 park facts that will **rock your world**

Some of the most eye-catching features you'll see in the national parks are rocks, boulders, cliffs, and arches. Most are millions of years old. Read on to discover amazing facts about park rocks!

1 The **oldest** rocks in the **Grand Canyon** are almost **two billion** years old.

2 The cliffs in **Pinnacles National Park** are moving **northward** at about a thumb length each year.

3 In **Arches** National Park there are more than **2,000** natural **rock arches.**

4 The mountains that make up **Guadalupe National Park** were once a coral reef in a **prehistoric ocean.**

5 It will be at least **50,000** years before the presidents' carved faces are worn away on **Mount Rushmore.**

BarkPark

Have you ever seen a dog that resembles its owner? Look for clues to figure out which canine belongs to which owner in this park.

Rangers at **Denali** use **Alaskan huskies,** or sled dogs, to patrol **two million acres** (809,371 ha) of the park where **vehicles** aren't allowed.

In some of **New York City's** ten national parks, you can even bring **Fido!** Leashed **dogs** are allowed on the national park trails near the city **harbor.**

CHECK YOUR ANSWERS ON PAGE 149.

TAKE A LOOK! BISCAYNE NATIONAL PARK

< FIND THESE **NATIONAL PARK** ITEMS >

3 puffer fish	6 sea stars	chest	1 ship's wheel
2 octopuses	1 sunken	2 scuba divers	3 sea turtles
3 crabs	treasure	3 rays	7 sharks

Fun Fact!

Off the coast of **Biscayne** National Park are **more** than **40** **shipwrecks.**

CHECK YOUR ANSWERS ON PAGE 149.

Was that a bear going over the mountain? In Great Smoky Mountains National Park, while you're enjoying the towering waterfalls, tranquil trails, and old log cabins, keep your eyes open for black bears—there are plenty out there!

Fun Fact! It is illegal to come within 50 yards (46 m)—about half the length of a football field—of a black bear in the park.

Great Smoky Mountains National Park

After we pick up our permits from the Great Smoky

Mountains park ranger _____ , we start to _____ along a narrow path.
                        type of building   *verb*

I'm just thinking what a(n) _____ place this is when the ranger suddenly yells out, "Hey,
                            adjective

_____ !" _____ and I stop and look at the ranger like he has a(n) _____
silly word   *friend's name*   *noun*

on his _____ . Then the ranger points into the woods. We see a(n) _____
        body part   *adjective*

_____ body part poking out from behind a tree. "Shhhh. Bears," the ranger whispers.
color

"If we stay really still and don't make any noise, we'll be able to see them _____ ."
                                                                            verb ending in –ing

We stay as still as a(n) _____ , but we don't see any more sign of the bears. We decide to
                        noun

_____ on down the path. Just as we turn a bend, we see them! One bear is _____
verb   *verb ending in –ing*

on a(n) _____ , while another does a(n) _____ . Two more look like they're
        noun   *gymnastics move*

playing _____ ! It looks like so much fun!
        name of a game

49

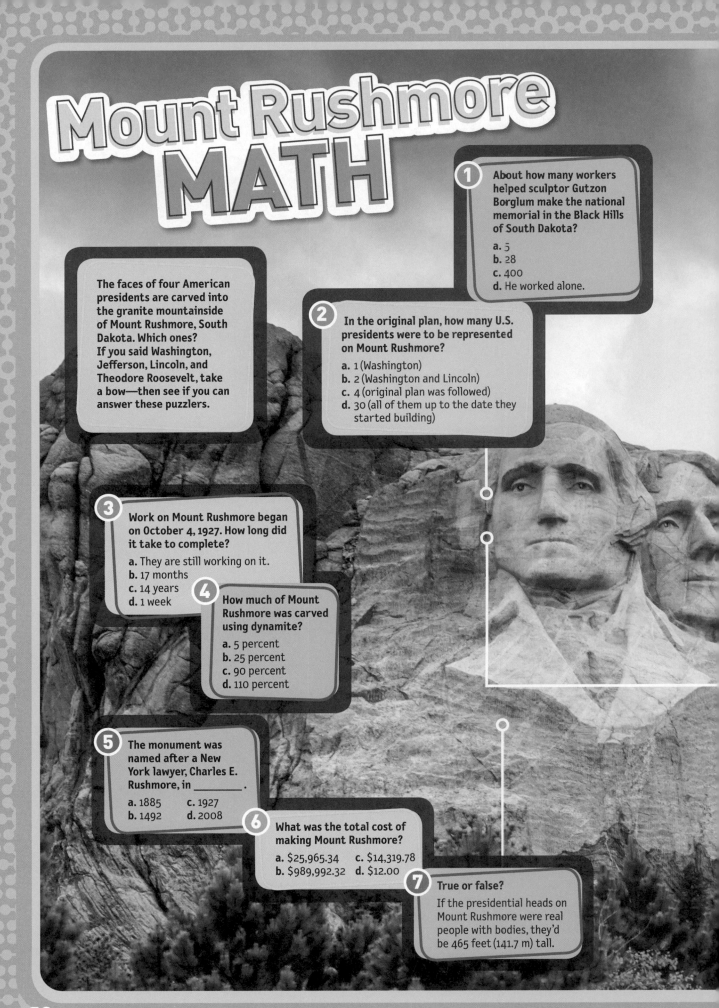

Mount Rushmore MATH

1 About how many workers helped sculptor Gutzon Borglum make the national memorial in the Black Hills of South Dakota?

a. 5
b. 28
c. 400
d. He worked alone.

The faces of four American presidents are carved into the granite mountainside of Mount Rushmore, South Dakota. Which ones? If you said Washington, Jefferson, Lincoln, and Theodore Roosevelt, take a bow—then see if you can answer these puzzlers.

2 In the original plan, how many U.S. presidents were to be represented on Mount Rushmore?

a. 1 (Washington)
b. 2 (Washington and Lincoln)
c. 4 (original plan was followed)
d. 30 (all of them up to the date they started building)

3 Work on Mount Rushmore began on October 4, 1927. How long did it take to complete?

a. They are still working on it.
b. 17 months
c. 14 years
d. 1 week

4 How much of Mount Rushmore was carved using dynamite?

a. 5 percent
b. 25 percent
c. 90 percent
d. 110 percent

5 The monument was named after a New York lawyer, Charles E. Rushmore, in _____ .

a. 1885   c. 1927
b. 1492   d. 2008

6 What was the total cost of making Mount Rushmore?

a. $25,965.34   c. $14,319.78
b. $989,992.32   d. $12.00

7 True or false?

If the presidential heads on Mount Rushmore were real people with bodies, they'd be 465 feet (141.7 m) tall.

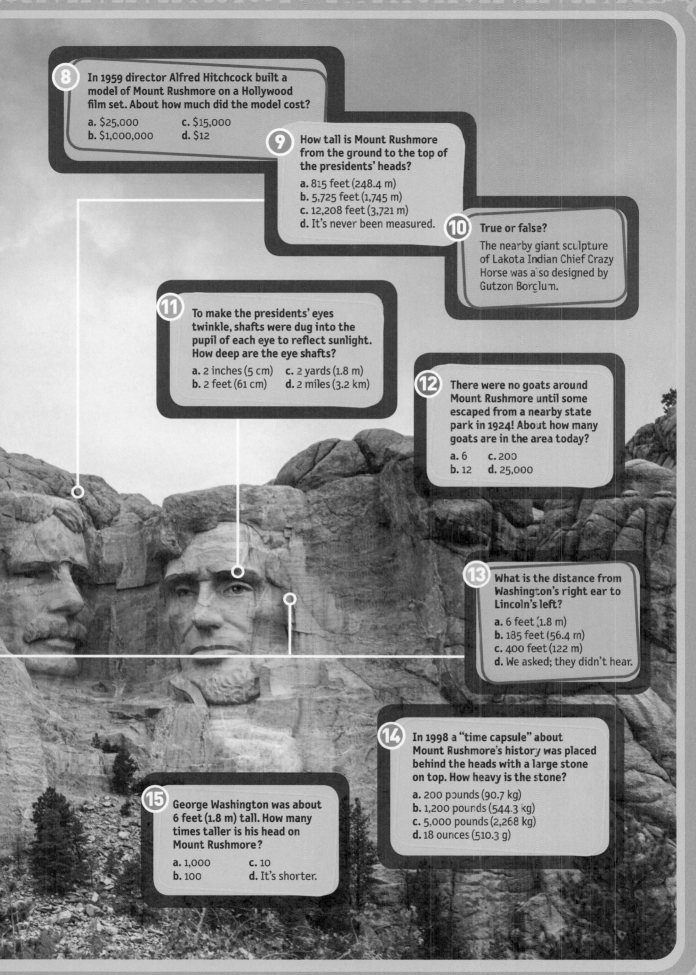

8 In 1959 director Alfred Hitchcock built a model of Mount Rushmore on a Hollywood film set. About how much did the model cost?

a. $25,000 c. $15,000
b. $1,000,000 d. $12

9 How tall is Mount Rushmore from the ground to the top of the presidents' heads?

a. 815 feet (248.4 m)
b. 5,725 feet (1,745 m)
c. 12,208 feet (3,721 m)
d. It's never been measured.

10 True or false?

The nearby giant sculpture of Lakota Indian Chief Crazy Horse was also designed by Gutzon Borglum.

11 To make the presidents' eyes twinkle, shafts were dug into the pupil of each eye to reflect sunlight. How deep are the eye shafts?

a. 2 inches (5 cm) c. 2 yards (1.8 m)
b. 2 feet (61 cm) d. 2 miles (3.2 km)

12 There were no goats around Mount Rushmore until some escaped from a nearby state park in 1924! About how many goats are in the area today?

a. 6 c. 200
b. 12 d. 25,000

13 What is the distance from Washington's right ear to Lincoln's left?

a. 6 feet (1.8 m)
b. 185 feet (56.4 m)
c. 400 feet (122 m)
d. We asked; they didn't hear.

14 In 1998 a "time capsule" about Mount Rushmore's history was placed behind the heads with a large stone on top. How heavy is the stone?

a. 200 pounds (90.7 kg)
b. 1,200 pounds (544.3 kg)
c. 5,000 pounds (2,268 kg)
d. 18 ounces (510.3 g)

15 George Washington was about 6 feet (1.8 m) tall. How many times taller is his head on Mount Rushmore?

a. 1,000 c. 10
b. 100 d. It's shorter.

CHECK YOUR ANSWERS ON PAGE 149.

Up, Up, and Away

Find the sky path that leads to the lost kite. Some paths may take you through grass, kites, clouds, and trees.

It used to be **illegal** to fly a kite on Washington, D.C.'s **National Mall.** But today, fliers unleash their strings for an **annual kite festival** every **spring.**

START

FINISH!

CHECK YOUR ANSWERS ON PAGE 149.

What in the World?

ANIMAL HEADGEAR

Can you recognize these national park residents by their headgear? Unscramble the letters to identify the critters in these close-ups.

NISBO

_____

LUAQI

_____

OSOME

_____

LUME ERDE

_____

OORPRNNGH

_____

ODRNHE ZARDLI

_____

CKWEEROODP

_____

ALDL HESEP

_____

GSTA TLEEEB

_____

CHECK YOUR ANSWERS ON PAGE 149.

Weird but true!

Amazing animal SENSES

Chances are, the animals in the parks will see or hear you before you discover them.

CHIPMUNKS SEE IN SLOW MOTION.

RABBITS can see behind them without moving their **HEADS.**

DOLPHINS can hear **SOUNDS** underwater **FROM 15** miles (24 km) **away.**

Beavers have a set of clear **eyelids** to see underwater.

A **LIZARD** sticks out its **TONGUE** to smell.

I'M JUST TAKING A WHIFF!

STUMP
YOUR PARENTS

When the adults in your family see wildlife, can they tell the males from the females? Test their knowledge with these questions.

1 Mountain goats live high in northern national parks such as Glacier and North Cascades. Males are called billies. Females are called _____ .
a. nannies
b. grannies
c. annies
d. zannies

2 The only species in the deer family in which both males and females grow antlers is_____ .
a. moose
b. elk
c. caribou
d. white-tailed deer

3 Wild turkeys can be seen in national parks from Acadia to the Everglades and across the western United States. Male turkeys gobble. What do female turkeys do?
a. gobble
b. growl
c. bark
d. click

4 True or false? Only female mosquitoes bite.

5 True or false? In most frog species, the males are larger than the females.

6 Male woodchucks are called he-chucks; females are called _____ .
a. hens
b. mares
c. jennies
d. she-chucks

7 Female rabbits are called does, and male rabbits are called _____ .
a. bucks
b. stallions
c. he-chucks
d. rams

8 True or false? Female barn swallows are attracted to males that have the longest and most symmetrical tails.

9 Among bighorn sheep—found in Rocky Mountain National Park (Colorado) and other mountainous areas—the horns of the males grow long, thick, and curved; the horns of the females are _____ .
a. forked with several branches
b. short and slightly curved
c. long, straight, and pointed
d. red

Funny Fill-In

Whenever you visit a national park, or even a national seashore, don't forget all your trash! Every year, volunteers pick up more than 150 tons (136 mt) of trash from Padre Island National Seashore in Texas. Do your part to protect our beaches.

Beach Patrol

My friend _____ and I volunteered for a beach cleanup. We stocked up on
                    friend's name

_____ trash bags and _____ gloves and headed for the shores of the
        adjective   adjective

_____ . We picked up _____ aluminum _____ ,
   body of water   large number   plural noun

_____ plastic, a soggy _____ sandwich, and a rusty _____ .
   adjective   food   type of transportation

Suddenly a(n) _____ wave _____ onto the beach and washed up a
                   adjective   past-tense verb

treasure chest covered with _____ . My heart started _____
                             beach item from nature, plural   verb ending in -ing

as we pried open the chest with a(n) _____ . There were at least _____
                                          noun   number

_____ coins inside! My friend and I yelled, "We're rich!" But when I scooped up some
   type of metal

of the coins, they _____ all over my hands. The coins turned out to be
                      past-tense verb

_____ wrapped in colored foil. But we had a great day anyway.
   type of candy, plural

Name That INSECT

There are 900,000 known insect species living on the planet, and scientists think there may be millions more we haven't yet named. Here are some common ones you might see in a park or preserve. Can you identify them?

A

These uninvited guests may show up to a picnic in almost any national park! They're found from coast to coast and have adapted to many different habitats. When crushed, they give off a foul odor.

B

With a migration of more than 3,000 miles (4,828 km), these orange-and-black insects make their way to their wintering grounds in southern California and Mexico, sometimes flying 100 miles (161 km) in a day.

It's a bug's life

Several hundred different kinds of insects live at Great Sand Dunes National Park and Preserve, Colorado. There are many spiders, too.

D

For two weeks each June in the Great Smoky Mountains National Park, thousands of these beetles gather at night and flash in unison.

C

Look for this insect in parks with plenty of grass. It can leap 20 times its body length—no wonder its jumping ability is part of its name.

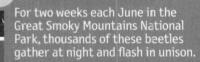

57
CHECK YOUR ANSWERS ON PAGE 150.

MAP MANIA!

AMAZING ALASKA

Head north to Alaska to see wilderness, glaciers, grizzlies, and more. Try answering these questions, then find the correct location for each park on this map of Alaska.

Alaska (U.S.)

U.S.

PACIFIC OCEAN

A

Yukon River

C

① WRANGELL-ST. ELIAS

This national park, the largest in the United States, _____ .

a. is six times the size of Yellowstone
b. contains the second tallest peak in the U.S.
c. has a wilderness area as large as Massachusetts and Connecticut combined
d. all of the above

② KOBUK VALLEY

True or false?
The 1,000 to 2,000 people who visit this park each year may see caribou, salmon, sand dunes, and arctic camels.

④ KATMAI

To keep the plentiful brown bears away from campers in this wild park on the Alaska Peninsula, the Brooks Camp campground is surrounded by _____ .

a. a moat
b. an electric fence
c. fast-food restaurants
d. high walls

③ GLACIER BAY

Park rangers lead boat tours around Glacier Bay, where visitors spot animals ashore, including _____ .

a. moose
b. bears
c. penguins
d. a and b

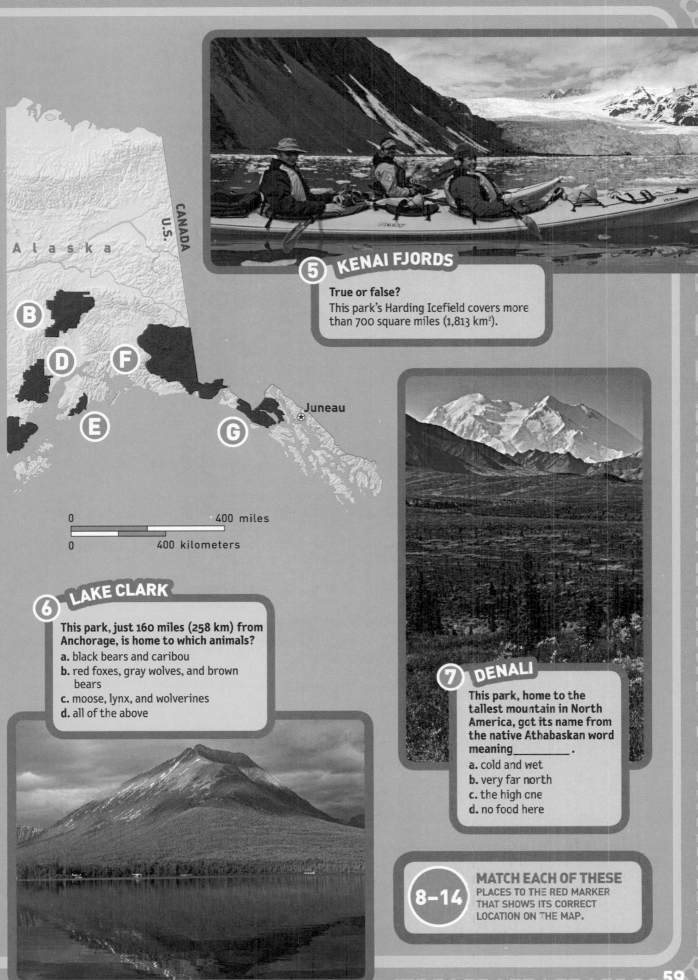

CANADA

U.S.

Alaska

B

D

F

E

G

Juneau ⊛

0   400 miles

0   400 kilometers

⑤ KENAI FJORDS

True or false?
This park's Harding Icefield covers more than 700 square miles (1,813 km³).

⑥ LAKE CLARK

This park, just 160 miles (258 km) from Anchorage, is home to which animals?
a. black bears and caribou
b. red foxes, gray wolves, and brown bears
c. moose, lynx, and wolverines
d. all of the above

⑦ DENALI

This park, home to the tallest mountain in North America, got its name from the native Athabaskan word meaning_____.
a. cold and wet
b. very far north
c. the high one
d. no food here

8–14 MATCH EACH OF THESE
PLACES TO THE RED MARKER THAT SHOWS ITS CORRECT LOCATION ON THE MAP.

59

CHECK YOUR ANSWERS ON PAGE 150.

Funny FILL-IN

For a sea-level look at Washington's Olympic National Park, try paddling in the Pacific. Just watch out for waves—and curious harbor seals! So grab your paddle and get ready to explore the great Pacific Northwest!

Fun Fact! Harbor seals move through water very quickly, but on land they have to bounce on their bellies to get around.

Olympic National Park

We're flying off to the Pacific coast in search of marine mammals. _____ (friend's name) and I can't wait to dip our _____ (body part, plural) into the ocean. When we get to the coast, we see people _____ (verb ending in –ing) through the waves on kayaks. So we put on our _____ (clothing item, plural), grab our _____ (noun, plural), and join them. We're paddling around a(n) _____ (adjective) rock when I look into the water and see something _____ (verb) past in the water below. It's a(n) _____ (adjective) harbor seal. It _____ (verb ending in –s) and rolls around in the water. Then it flaps its _____ (body part) at me, and I get soaked! Suddenly I'm surrounded by _____ (large number) seals that _____ (verb) and _____ (verb) through the water. We finish kayaking for the day, and as we _____ (verb) along the coast we see _____ (adjective) seals lying on the _____ (noun, plural). They aren't moving too _____ (adverb ending in –ly) now that they're on land, but I think I see one of them wave its _____ (body part) at me.

60

5 fun facts about flicks filmed in parks

Are you a film fan? You might recognize some national park scenes from the movies!

1 In the *Star Wars* movie *Return of the Jedi,* some scenes of **ewoks** on planet Endor were filmed in **Redwood National Park.**

2 Segments of *Transformers: Revenge of the Fallen* were **filmed** at the Smithsonian **National Air and Space Museum.** Props used in the film are on **display** there.

3 For some scenes in *Star Wars: A New Hope,* Death Valley played the part of Luke Skywalker's desert **planet Tatooine.**

4 The 2014 Disney movie **BEARS,** documenting a year in the life of a bear family, was filmed in several **Alaska** national parks.

5 The sandstone arches that appear in *Indiana Jones and the Last Crusade* are Double Arch in Arches National Park, **Utah.**

The EVERGLADES

The 1,508,537-acre (610,483-ha) Everglades is a vast wilderness that hosts an amazing variety of plants and animals. Test your Everglades expertise here.

1 What is the name of this popular mode of transportation to explore the Everglades?
a. airboat
c. surfboard
b. watertruck
d. ferry

2 What U.S. president dedicated Everglades National Park in 1947?
a. Harry S. Truman
c. John F. Kennedy
b. Abraham Lincoln
d. Ronald Reagan

3 In what U.S. state is the Everglades located?
a. California
c. Florida
b. Mississippi
d. Alaska

4 What invasive species has been attacking the native wildlife of the Everglades?
a. leatherback sea turtle
b. Key deer
c. Burmese python
d. kangaroo

5 Who were some of the first people to call the Everglades home?
a. Calusa Indians
c. Vikings
b. Spanish explorers
d. English colonists

6 The mangrove trees help protect the Everglades from _____.
a. animal invaders
b. the sun's UV rays
c. hurricane storm surges
d. traffic

7 **True or false?** The American alligator of the Everglades has sensors all over its body that can detect motion in the water.

American alligator

8 Saltwater and freshwater come together in an area called _____.
a. an estuary   **c.** a lake
b. a bay   **d.** a waterfall

9 Which Everglades-dwelling animal is endangered?
a. Florida panther   **c.** wood stork
b. West Indian manatee **d.** all of the above

10 What nickname is often used for the Everglades?
a. Old Man River   **c.** River of Grass
b. Rumbling Waters   **d.** Waterloo

11 Which plant, found in the Everglades, is named for its sharp edge?
a. Venus fly trap
b. sawgrass
c. prickly pear cactus
d. poinsettia

12 Which plant wraps itself around other trees in the Everglades to rob them of sunlight and nutrients?
a. strangler fig
b. weeping willow
c. dragon tree
d. monkey puzzle tree

13 **True or false?** The Everglades never experiences a dry season.

Mangrove trees

Just Joking

The red fox is the largest fox species. It is found in national parks throughout North America.

KNOCK, KNOCK.

Who's there?
Mikey.
Mikey who?
Mikey doesn't work. Can you open the door?

HA HAHA!

JEFF: Did you enjoy your camping trip even though it was raining?
MARY: It was in-tents.

What do you call an alligator eating Mexican **food?** Q

A Tacodile. A

What do you call **a borrowed** Q **bison?**

A buff-a-loan. A

Name That ROCK

Whether you're kicking a small one down the road or climbing a gigantic one at the park, rocks are all around you, and they shape your world. Can you identify the rocks on this page?

A This durable rock often forms massive cliffs, peaks, and domes, as in Yosemite National Park.

B The stone arches in Arches National Park were formed when rainwater dissolved the softer parts of this rock over many years.

C Often used in saunas, because it is not damaged by repeated heating and cooling, this mineral is found in Mount Rainier National Park.

D Some of the oldest fossils found on Earth are preserved in this soft sedimentary rock in Grand Canyon National Park.

Rock towers

In The Needles district of Canyonlands National Park, Utah, the sandstone has been eroded into spectacular tall red-and-tan spires.

CHECK YOUR ANSWERS ON PAGE 150.

dive iN

Dolphin groups, called pods, **swim** in the oceans **in and around** national parks from **Hawaii** to **Florida.**

Help the bottlenose dolphin mother and baby swim to the family reunion. Only one path through the sea will get them to the big family get-together!

staRt

finiSh

What in the World?

ALOHA ADVENTURE

Is Hawaii on your horizon? Will you find a rare honeycreeper in Haleakalā or see spewing lava at Hawai'i Volcanoes? Visit military memorials or hear traditional tunes? Unscramble the letters below these zoomed-in photos of Hawaiian attractions. Watch out—some of the words are Hawaiian!

NRAI RESFOT

_____

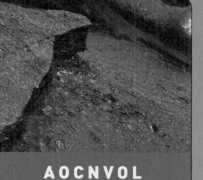

AOCNVOL

_____

ESA LEURTT

_____

AATLERFLW

_____

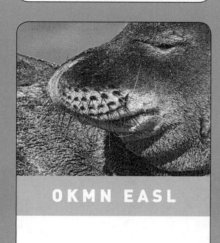

OKMN EASL

_____

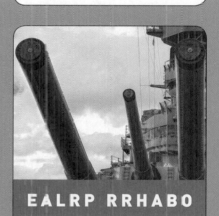

EALRP RRHABO

_____

QOUIC GFOR

_____

OKA ETRE

_____

A'OHI EHLUA

_____

CHECK YOUR ANSWERS ON PAGE 150.

RANGER TIPS

FUN THINGS TO DO

Build a sand castle
Make a bark rubbing
Make a flower chain
Make a pressed flower
Make rock art
Make a shell design
Study pond animals
Collect leaves

In national parks, you can go on fungus forays, measure trees, identify insects, and do other outdoor activities. But be sure to look after nature.

- don't litter
- don't pick wildflowers
- don't disturb animals

Have a great time, enjoy yourself, and keep safe!

10 ESSENTIAL THINGS TO BRING

Whatever activity or adventure you plan to do, here are some basic items that will be useful to bring.

maps _____
water _____
sun hat _____
sunglasses _____
binoculars _____
field guide _____
notebook and pen _____
cell phone _____
compass _____
a snack _____

ACTIVITY CHECKLIST

I have done the following things in a national park.

Hiking _____
Cycling _____
Swimming _____
Bird-watching _____
Tree identification _____
Camping _____
Rock climbing _____
Sailing _____
Camp cooking _____
Canoeing _____

Funny Fill-IN

Choose your adventure in Yosemite National Park! Will you hike Half Dome or gaze up at giant sequoias? No matter what you do, your visit won't be complete without a glimpse of awesome wild animals that roam the park. What are you waiting for? Get out there!

Fun Fact! In 1881, a tunnel was drilled through a giant sequoia tree in Yosemite. Cars could drive right through the tree!

Yosemite National Park

As soon as we arrive in Yosemite in California,

we rent _____ and _____ through the park. At Mariposa Grove,
　　　　　 type of animal, plural 　　　　 verb

we see _____ sequoia trees that are so huge a car could _____ right through
　　　　 adjective 　　　　　　　　　　　　　　　　　　　　　　 verb

them! Above us _____ squirrels _____ and jump from branch to _____ .
　　　　　　　　 color 　　　　　　 verb 　　　　　　　　　　　　　　 noun

I drop my backpack onto a(n) _____ and get right up close to one of the trees.
　　　　　　　　　　　　　　 noun

I try hard to wrap my _____ around the tree trunk, but I would need to be
　　　　　　　　　　　 body part, plural

_____ to reach! When I see _____ posing like _____ ,
adjective ending in –er 　　　　　　 friend's name 　　　　　 name of a pop star

I _____ and reach for my backpack to get my _____ camera. But my backpack
　 verb 　　　　　　　　　　　　　　　　　　　 adjective

is missing! The park ranger looks _____ , shakes his _____ , and says, "Rule
　　　　　　　　　　　　　　　　　 feeling 　　　　　　　 body part

number _____ : Never leave your backpack unattended. But don't be _____ ;
　　　　 number 　　　　　　　　　　　　　　　　　　　　　　　　　　　　 feeling

some friends have found it, and they will hand it in at the park office."

69

Trading Places

These animals wandered into the wrong national parks! Can you fix this mess? Write each animal's name (listed below) next to its proper habitat. Hint: Some parks have more than one habitat, so pay attention to the habitat named at the top of each photo.

- sea star
- happy face spider
- black bear
- golden eagle
- chuckwalla lizard

1
Coral reef
Virgin Islands

2
Forest
Yosemite

3 Desert
Death Valley

4 Rain forest
Hawaii

5 Rocky cliffs
Grand Canyon

Dive and Discover

These two underwater scenes may look alike, but they aren't the same. See if you can find and circle the 20 differences.

Dry Tortugas National Park in Florida is **99 percent** water, with just **seven** tiny islands of coral and **sand.**

Virgin Islands National Park features a **225-yard** (206-m)- long underwater snorkeling **trail.**

13579

13578

Name That TRACK

Sometimes it's hard to spot park animals. If you can't find them, look for their tracks in soft dirt, mud, or snow. You might find animal tracks near food sources—like berry bushes—or water. Can you identify these tracks?

A This five-inch (13-cm)-wide paw print with four toes above the pad belongs to one oversize kitty found in such parks as Bryce Canyon.

B These tracks belong to a large, furry creature that lives in the woods of many parks. Its hind feet are wider but shorter than an adult human's feet, and its claws are much sharper.

C The tracks of this common black, feathered creature may be found on the ground, but you listen for its caw overhead.

Keep on tracking

In Yellowstone you can find tracks of 67 species of mammals—including bears, moose, mountain lions, bighorn sheep, and buffalo. Just remember to keep your distance from wildlife!

D Olympic National Park in Washington is just one of the many national parks that are home to the masked creature that left these tracks. Its five fingers are capable of turning knobs and opening jars.

CHECK YOUR ANSWERS ON PAGE 151.

Wacky forces of nature

The Statue of Liberty's torch **sways** up to 5 inches (12.7 cm) **in the wind.**

I'VE BEEN HOLDING UP THIS TORCH SINCE 1886!

There's weird and way-out natural stuff happening at some national parks!

DEATH VALLEY, California, is the hottest place in **NORTH AMERICA.**

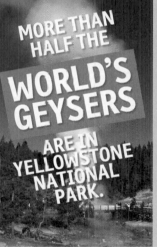

MORE THAN HALF THE **WORLD'S GEYSERS** ARE IN YELLOWSTONE NATIONAL PARK.

Nighttime **rainbows** are common at Yosemite National Park.

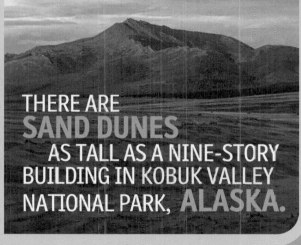

THERE ARE SAND DUNES AS TALL AS A NINE-STORY BUILDING IN KOBUK VALLEY NATIONAL PARK, ALASKA.

What in the World?

ASTONISHING SHENANDOAH

Oh, Shenandoah! Seventy-five miles (121 km) west of Washington, D.C., Shenandoah National Park invites visitors to enjoy the Blue Ridge Mountains. Unscramble the letters beneath these zoomed-in photos to identify park features and residents.

TELYBUTRF

_____

ODDENGOLR

_____

EDR ERLAMNSAAD

_____

INUNTAMO LALURE

_____

DRE XFO

_____

UEBL YJA

_____

RGAVIINI EEERRPC

_____

ATBCBO

_____

AOORCCN

_____

CHECK YOUR ANSWERS ON PAGE 151.

Bet you didn't know

5 incredible facts about trees

In the national parks you might find trees you've never seen before. Check out these tremendous facts about trees.

1 A bristlecone pine tree in Great Basin National Park, Nevada, lived nearly **5,000 years** before it was cut down.

2 A **redwood tree** can produce up to **100,000** seeds in a year.

3 **Petrified** wood made from fossilized trees at Petrified Forest National Park is almost **solid quartz.** You can cut it only with a diamond-tipped **saw!**

4 The world's tallest tree— a redwood named **Hyperion**— stands somewhere in Redwood National Park. Scientists won't reveal its exact **location.**

5 Hawai'i Volcanoes National Park is home to **15** species of **endangered** trees.

MAP MANIA!
BATTLE-FIELDS

Bullets, battlegrounds, bastions, and bulwarks—the national parks preserve many military milestones of U.S. history. Test your battle-readiness by answering these questions, and then match each event to the corresponding site on the map.

1 WHERE WAR BEGAN

Confederate forces attacked Fort Sumter on April 12, 1861, signaling the start of the_____.

a. summer
b. Civil War
c. War of 1812
d. Patriot War

2 CUSTER'S LAST STAND

In this 1876 battle, Crazy Horse and other Lakota Sioux and Cheyenne warriors defeated the U.S. Army Seventh Calvary, led by Col. George Custer, near the_____.

a. Little Bighorn River
b. Big Littlehorn Swamp
c. Last Chance Gulch
d. Dead Man's Gulch

3 BATTLE OF BUNKER HILL

This was a significant early battle of_____.

a. the Revolutionary War
b. the Civil War
c. World War I
d. the Navajo Wars

4 PATRIOTIC PRIDE

In a battle during the War of 1812, British ships bombarded Fort McHenry in Baltimore Harbor. When Francis Scott Key saw the American flag still flying over the fort the next morning, he was inspired to write_____.

a. "The Battle Hymn of the Republic"
b. "This Land Is Your Land"
c. "The Star-Spangled Banner"
d. "America the Beautiful"

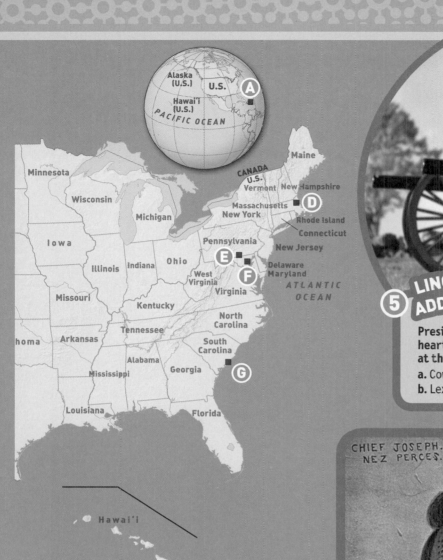

⑤ LINCOLN'S ADDRESS

President Lincoln delivered brief, heartfelt, and now famous remarks at this Civil War battlefield.

a. Cowpens   c. Gettysburg
b. Lexington   d. Appomattox

CHIEF JOSEPH. NEZ PERCES.

⑥ SPANISH HERITAGE

In 1539, the Spanish built a strong fort—El Morro—on an island in San Juan Bay, Puerto Rico. The fort was attacked by _____.

a. Sir Francis Drake in 1595
b. the Dutch in 1625
c. the United States in 1898
d. all of the above

⑦ NEZ PERCE WAR

True or false?
The Nez Perce people were heading toward Mexico when they were stopped by the U.S. Army in 1877.

8–14 MATCH EACH OF THESE

PARKS RELATED TO EACH STORY TO THE RED MARKER THAT SHOWS ITS CORRECT LOCATION ON THE MAP.

79

TAKE A LOOK! ACADIA NATIONAL PARK

< FIND THESE **NATIONAL PARK** ITEMS >

7 birds	2 kayakers	1 shell
2 squirrels	1 tent	6 seals
12 people	2 lobsters	

Fun Fact!

During the summer at Acadia, go on a whale-watching **trip** to see humpback **whales,** which occasionally leap right out of the **water!**

CHECK YOUR ANSWERS ON PAGE 151.

Just Joking

You can ride a horse through some national parks, such as Yellowstone, Petrified Forest, and Joshua Tree.

KNOCK, KNOCK.

Who's there?
Ears
Ears who?
Ears another joke for you.

TONGUE TWISTER!

Say this fast three times:

A noise annoys an oyster.

You've got to be joking ...

Q Why do **birds** fly south?

A Because it is too far to walk.

JIM: Why would anyone want to meet a skunk?
NANCY: Because a skunk is an animal of great dis-stink-tion.

TONGUE TWISTER!

Say this fast three times:

Randy rode a raft down a rapid, rushing river.

STUMP
YOUR PARENTS

National parks are about arts too! Many park sites honor and preserve the heritage of American artists, arts, and artifacts. Can you or your parents answer these questions about arts in the parks?

1 **True or false?**
In Yosemite National Park there's a peak named for the landscape photographer Ansel Adams.

2 **The Wayside residence in Minute Man National Historical Park, Massachusetts, was once home to which author?**
a. Louisa May Alcott
b. Nathaniel Hawthorne
c. Margaret Sidney
d. all of the above

3 **At Wolf Trap National Park for the Performing Arts, Virginia, visitors may _____ .**
a. hunt wolves   **c.** see puppet shows
b. camp   **d.** swim

4 **Augustus Saint-Gaudens, whose sculpture-filled New Hampshire home is preserved as a national historic site, was a famous_____ .**
a. actor   **c.** artist
b. poet   **d.** senator

5 **At national parks, including Petrified Forest and Saguaro in Arizona, you can see rock engravings left by native peoples. These pictures on the rocks are called _____ .**
a. rockets
b. petroglyphs
c. graphic novels
d. none of the above

6 **In Yellowstone National Park, an area of multicolored mineral springs and mud pots is named for the hues of an artist's palette. What's it called?**
a. Artist Paint Pots   **c.** Rainbow Bridge
b. Mr. Pricklepants   **d.** Colormaker

7 **The home of Edgar Allan Poe, who wrote *The Tell-Tale Heart* and many other scary stories, is a national historic site in Philadelphia. Visitors there are greeted by a sculpture of a _____ .**
a. book and candle   **c.** ghost
b. raven   **d.** dragon

8 **True or false?**
In Kings Canyon National Park, you can see murals showing Native American life painted in 1947 by the celebrated Hopi artist Fred Kabotie.

9 **The Statue of Liberty was a gift of friendship to the United States from the people of _____ .**
a. Egypt   **c.** China
b. Mexico   **d.** France

CHECK YOUR ANSWERS ON PAGE 151.

Funny Fill-In

At Hawai'i Volcanoes National Park, get ready for spewing steam, flowing lava, and erupting ash. Home to two of the world's most active volcanoes—Mauna Loa and Kilauea—this park is constantly changing. Combined with Hawaii's amazing animals and plants, who knows what you might discover there!

Fun Fact! Thanks to the conservation efforts of park rangers, the nēnē goose, Hawaii's endangered state bird, has been brought back from the brink of extinction.

Hawai'i Volcanoes National Park

We're going to _____ around Kilauea, one of
                         verb

the _____ volcanoes that created the Hawaiian Islands. The park ranger tells us
       adjective

that Kilauea is one of the most active and _____ volcanoes in the world. We're
                                              adjective

driving down the road when suddenly the _____ ranger slams on the brakes.
                                            adjective

He _____ out the door and takes off like a(n) _____! "It's a nēnē
   verb ending in –s   *fast-moving animal*

goose," the park ranger says, escorting the bird off the road. "It's Hawaii's state bird, and

it's endangered." The park ranger is just about to tell us what we'll see at Kilauea, but

then he takes off again! He's _____ like _____. He takes a(n)
                               verb ending in –ing   *name of a superhero*

_____ leap and lands in front of a(n) _____ turtle. "Endangered hawksbill
   adjective   *adjective*

turtle!" the ranger gasps. We watch as the turtle _____ across the road.
                                                     verb ending in –s

_____! These rangers take their job seriously!
   exclamation

Name That LEAF

In the parks, it can be tricky figuring out what each plant is, but their leaves can give you a clue. Can you name the plants that match these leaves?

A These leaves belong to a tree that delivers something sweet to your breakfast table. Most common in the northeastern states, it puts on a colorful show in the fall.

B With little "teeth" around its edges, you'd think this leaf had a bite. The slightest breeze makes the leaves of this tree—found in cooler areas and mountains across North America— shudder. That shudder gives you a clue to the tree's name.

C As a general rule, these leaves on a bush grow in clusters of three. The bush is found along trails, streams, or meadows throughout the United States. Just remember: You can look, but don't touch. This leaf can leave you itching!

D You might use these prickly, dark green leaves and bright red berries for winter decorations . You're most likely to see this tree in the southeastern United States, but it grows as far north as Massachusetts.

All fall down

The average maple tree drops 600,000 leaves every fall.

CHECK YOUR ANSWERS ON PAGE 152.

Grand Teton Adventure

Help the visitors, at top left, in Grand Teton National Park in Wyoming find the park ranger while avoiding the people, animals, and other obstacles blocking their path.

START

GRAND TETON NATIONAL PARK

END

CHECK YOUR ANSWERS ON PAGE 152.

Find the
HIDDEN ANIMALS

A

B

On the land and in the sea, how many creatures can you see? Many animals hide by blending into their surroundings. Find the listed animals in these photos, and write the letter of the correct picture next to each animal name.

1. praying mantis _____
2. moon jellyfish _____
3. sphinx moth _____
4. goldenrod crab spider _____
5. grouse _____

C

D

E

CHECK YOUR ANSWERS ON PAGE 152.

Bet you didn't know

5 park facts to listen to

For more than a decade, the National Park Service has been recording sounds in its parks to measure human and natural sounds. What can you hear? Sound off with these fun facts.

1 Elk make "bugle" sounds in Rocky Mountain National Park.

2 About 25 percent of sounds a national park visitor hears is noise caused by humans.

3 Certain sand dunes occasionally hum. Listen closely when you visit Great Sand Dunes National Park!

4 The common coqui is the loudest amphibian. When groups croak together, they can be as loud as a lawn mower!

5 The western diamondback rattlesnake can vibrate its rattle about 60 times a second.

87

What in the World?

NTTE

_____

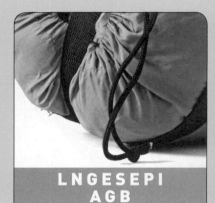

LNGESEPI AGB

_____

CSPASOM

_____

ISSSW MYAR NFEKPENI

_____

AACCBKKP

_____

APCMREFI

_____

YNGFRI NPA

_____

INRSLAOBCU

_____

ALFLIGHSHT

_____

Funny Fill-In

Dive into the amazing watery world of the National Park of American Samoa. This park—whose name means "sacred earth"—protects a diverse coral reef, teeming with tropical fish, dolphins, and sea turtles. So strap on your snorkel and get ready to explore under the waves.

Scuba Surprise

On our last day, we all went scuba _____ . We _____ off
                             verb ending in -ing   past-tense verb

the _____ wearing _____ _____ . Under the
         noun   adjective   article of clothing, plural

_____ water, I came face-to-face with a(n) _____ creature
  adjective   adjective

with the head of a(n) _____ and the body of a(n) _____ ! It had
              land animal   water animal

_____ _____ covered in _____ stripes. "Hi," the
large number   body part, plural   color

creature said. "My name is _____ ." Then it _____ at me. I turned to
                 celebrity   past-tense verb

get my family's attention, but the creature swam away faster than a(n) _____ !
                                                       noun

Clearly I had discovered a new species.

89

A DISTINCT DESERT

The spectacular Sonoran Desert lies in Mexico, Arizona, and California. You can see parts of this complex North American desert in national parks from Saguaro in Arizona to Joshua Tree in California. Test your desert knowledge here!

1 Which of these living things is found only in the Sonoran Desert, which stretches across parts of the southwestern United States and northwest Mexico?

a. saguaro cactus
b. jackrabbit
c. monitor lizard
d. desert bloodwood tree

2 True or false? A person bitten by a desert rattlesnake will need about 20 vials of antivenom, or venom antidote.

3 The Sonoran Desert covers how much land?

a. 10,000 square miles (26,000 km²)
b. 42,000 square miles (109,000 km²)
c. 100,000 square miles (259,000 km²)
d. 54,000 square miles (140,000 km²)

4 True or false? Javelinas, pig-like creatures found in the Sonoran Desert, have a pleasant smell.

5 One desert plant, called the creosote bush, is one of the _____ plants in the world.

a. oldest
b. prickliest
c. smelliest
d. smallest

6 The saguaro cactus flower is the state flower of which southwestern state in the United States?

a. Oklahoma
b. California
c. Arizona
d. Texas

7 How does the desert wren use the cactus to stay alive?

a. It hangs its food on the cactus's spines.
b. It lives inside the trunk of the cactus.
c. It sits on top of the cactus to watch for prey.
d. It lays its eggs in the roots of the cactus.

Cacti in the sonoran desert

8 How much rain can an area get per year in order to be called a desert?
a. less than 1 inch (2.5 cm)
b. less than 10 inches (25 cm)
c. less than 20 inches (50 cm)
d. less than 50 inches (127 cm)

9 How much of Earth's land surface is covered by desert?
a. one-fifth
b. one-fourth
c. one-third
d. one-half

10 True or false? About 2,500 different kinds of edible plants grow in the Sonoran Desert.

11 Which U.S. desert is not a subregion of the Sonoran Desert?
a. Yuma Desert
b. Colorado Desert
c. Mojave Desert
d. Tonopah Desert

13 How long do saguaro cacti, which are native to the Sonoran Desert, typically live?
a. 40–50 years
b. 80–120 years
c. 150–200 years
d. 300–350 years

12 True or false? Summertime temperatures at the southern part of the Sonoran Desert can reach 134°F (57°C) in the shade.

14 The gila monster is the _____ lizard in the United States.
a. fastest
b. largest
c. smallest
d. deadliest

CHECK YOUR ANSWERS ON PAGE 152.

Double Take

See if you can spot 13 differences in the two pictures below.

Mount Rushmore National Monument, South Dakota

CHECK YOUR ANSWERS ON PAGE 152.

Reptile facts you can chew on

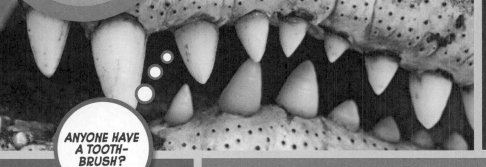

Everglades National Park is the only place on Earth where the American alligator and the American crocodile coexist.

ANYONE HAVE A TOOTH-BRUSH?

An **alligator** grows about **3,000 TEETH** in a lifetime.

CROCODILES HAVE BEEN AROUND FOR ABOUT **200 MILLION YEARS.**

Baby alligators **bark** when they are ready to **hatch** out of their **eggs.**

CROCODILES **CAN'T** CHEW.

Large **CROCODILES** can survive for more than a year **WITHOUT EATING.**

Name That BEACH ANIMAL

National park beaches are great places to see all kinds of animals. Do you know the names of these?

A This shorebird is big, colorful, long-legged, long-billed, and limited in range to the parks of Florida.

B A program at Biscayne National Park protects beaches where this threatened species nests. You'll recognize this sea turtle by its very large head.

C Descended from domestic animals that returned to the wild in the 17th century, these tough creatures have adapted and thrived. Two famous herds populate the remote and windswept stretches of Assateague Island National Seashore, in Maryland and Virginia.

D Related to spiders, this creature—often seen on Atlantic coast beaches—looks very similar to its prehistoric ancestors, which first appeared more than 300 million years ago (100 million years before dinosaurs).

Animal trackers

At the Point Reyes National Seashore, park managers installed wildlife cameras to monitor the local harbor seal population.

CHECK YOUR ANSWERS ON PAGE 152.

STUMP
YOUR PARENTS

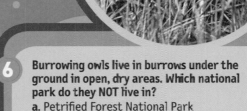

Raptors are birds of prey. Pinnacles (California), Rocky Mountain (Colorado), and other national parks protect raptor nesting areas. Answer these raptor questions.

1 When hiking in the woods, you may come across an owl pellet. What is it?
a. owl poop
b. owl vomit, or coughed-up food
c. an egg
d. a ball of soft feathers

2 The U.S. national bird is the bald eagle, but what did Benjamin Franklin want it to be?
a. hawk
b. dove
c. owl
d. turkey

3 What humans can see from 5 feet (1.5 m), hawks can see:
a. with their eyes closed
b. from 20 feet (6 m)
c. from 2 feet (61 cm)
d. with binoculars

4 True or false?
Golden eagles have been known to attack deer.

5 Soaring above treetops, the turkey vulture locates dead prey by using its sense of
_____.
a. vision
b. hearing
c. smell
d. echolocation

6 Burrowing owls live in burrows under the ground in open, dry areas. Which national park do they NOT live in?
a. Petrified Forest National Park
b. Theodore Roosevelt National Park
c. Acadia National Park
d. Sand Creek Massacre National Historic Site

7 Owl feathers have a special shape that allows the bird to _____.
a. swim underwater
b. fly silently
c. survive forest fires
d. time travel

8 True or false?
Bald eagles can swim.

9 Peregrine falcons, the fastest-flying birds in the world, swoop down to grab their prey in midair, flying at speeds of :
a. 15 miles an hour (24 km/h)
b. 200 miles an hour (322 km/h)
c. the speed of sound
d. warp speed

CHECK YOUR ANSWERS ON PAGE 153.

GRAND GETAWAY

It's vacation time in the amazing Grand Canyon! Join the fun by finding the 15 items below.

1. soccer ball
2. red sunglasses
3. sunscreen
4. golden retriever
5. blue-and-yellow tent
6. backward baseball cap
7. striped T-shirt
8. playing cards
9. ice-cream cone
10. umbrella
11. hot dog
12. green headband
13. postcard
14. map
15. flashlight

Funny FILL-IN

On a clear night in Death Valley National Park, the night sky turns into a ceiling of twinkling stars. Look up to see planets, constellations, and maybe even a meteor shower. What will you see up above the desert?

Death Valley National Park

When the park ranger asks us if we want to stargaze at night in Death Valley, we say "_____" right away! There are so many
<small>silly word</small>
stars here that we can even see the _____ galaxy. I'm lying on the ground,
<small>your teacher's name</small>
dreaming that I'm _____ exploring _____ , when suddenly a
<small>famous explorer</small> <small>name of a country</small>
bat _____ overhead and I nearly _____ out of my skin. Next, a spooky
<small>verb ending in –s</small> <small>verb</small>
_____ echoes all around us. Coyotes! _____ and I _____ in
<small>animal sound</small> <small>friend's name</small> <small>verb</small>
fear! Then we smell _____ . It's a spotted skunk! I'm about to grab a(n) _____
<small>something gross</small> <small>noun</small>
for protection, when a desert-banded gecko runs up my _____ . I _____ when
<small>body part</small> <small>verb</small>
I see a black widow spider on the _____—that gecko saved my life! When we
<small>same noun</small>
 finally get back to our lodge for the night, I notice that the gecko has followed us. So we

invite it in, and we settle back to watch the old Western playing on TV.

Just Joking

Elephant seals are named for the trunk-like snout that extends from the male's head. Look for them at Point Reyes National Seashore.

KNOCK, KNOCK.

Who's there?
Havasu
Havasu who?
Havasu call me.

JIM: Why was the grizzly turned away from the restaurant?

NANCY: No bear feet allowed.

TONGUE TWISTER!

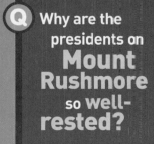

Say this fast three times:

Sick salamanders sipped and slurped soup.

ZZZZ...
ZZZZ... ZZZZ...
ZZZZ... ZZZZ
... ZZZZ

You've **got** to be joking ...

Q Why are the presidents on **Mount Rushmore** so **well-rested?**

A They sleep like rocks.

Name That FEATHER

What's that plume on the ground? Can you figure out which national park bird dropped which feather?

The background image shows breast feathers of the California quail.

A
These feathers can be up to 16 inches (40 cm) long and make good Thanksgiving decorations. They show up in woods and meadows in every state except Alaska.

B
Easy to spot on the forest floor, this feather can be found throughout eastern and central North America. The loud shriek of "Jay! Jay!" tells you who it belongs to.

C
This feather belongs to a bird that hunts at night in eastern woodlands and the Pacific Northwest. If you hear it, you might think it's asking, "Who cooks for you?"

D
Like the bird, this feather is seen only occasionally in parks to the west of the Rockies. The bird acts like a woodpecker, but it is not one.

On migration

More than 300 different kinds of birds can be found at Death Valley National Park. The terrain there creates a natural "funnel" that leads many migratory birds to pass through the park.

CHECK YOUR ANSWERS ON PAGE 153.

Funny Fill-In

Try an Acadia adventure! This park packs heaps of fabulous features into a small area—mostly on a single island. You can climb rocks, observe birds, or pick blueberries. Then hit the water for kayaking, whale-watching—or treasure hunting!

Fun Fact! Cadillac Mountain in Acadia National Park is the highest point along the East Coast of the United States.

Acadia National Park

We _____ all the way to the Atlantic coast to visit
                verb

this park's Mount Desert Island in Maine. When we get to the park's _____ , the
                                                                        noun

park ranger tells us we're going to have a(n) _____ time today, because we get to
                                                    adjective

_____ around the islands in a sailboat, exploring the coast. Near Baker Island, I see
    verb

something _____ in the water. It's a harbor porpoise! It has something _____
              adjective   adjective

on its _____ . Is that a(n) _____ like _____ wears?
        body part   something expensive   famous pop star

Then I see a(n) _____ whale float by with a(n) _____ . But things
                    adjective   cooking utensil

get really strange when a dolphin swims by with a(n) _____ . That's when the park
                                                          type of toy

ranger explains that there are shipwrecks in these waters. These animals must have been

_____ for treasure at a wreck. I wonder if there are any golden _____
verb ending in –ing   noun, plural

or a priceless _____ on the seabed just waiting to be discovered!
                    noun

5 fun facts to bear in mind

Bears are found in nearly one-third of all the national parks.

1 Many **brown bears** that live in North America are also called **grizzly bears.**

2 A **grizzly bear** can sniff out food **18 miles** (29 km) away.

3 Bears do **not** go to the bathroom **for months** while they're **hibernating.**

4 Male **black bears** can have a home range as large as **80** square miles (207 km²).

5 A **grizzly bear** can run as **fast** as a horse.

RANGER TIPS

A wintertime visit to a national park can be wonderful. Most of the crowds have gone home, so you'll have space to stretch out, enjoy some snow, and try new activities.

KEEP WARM IN WINTER

1. Dress in layers.
2. Wear a hat and mittens.
3. Keep your ears covered.
4. Wear waterproof boots big enough so you can wiggle your toes inside.
5. Take breaks to go inside, have a warm drink, and get dry clothes if you need them.

TOP FIVE NATIONAL PARKS FOR CROSS-COUNTRY SKIING

1. Acadia (Maine)
2. Bryce Canyon (Utah)
3. Cuyahoga (Ohio)
4. Glacier (Montana)
5. Grand Teton (Wyoming)

FIVE SUPER SNOW ACTIVITIES

1. Sledging
2. Skiing
3. Snowshoeing
4. Snowboarding
5. Building snow sculptures

TOP THREE EXTREME ICE ACTIVITIES

1. Go ice fishing (Glacier National Park or Acadia National Park).
2. Explore icy caves filled with icicles (Apostle Islands National Seashore, Wisconsin, or Lava Beds National Monument, California).
3. Learn how to do ice climbing—or watch the ice climbers (Glacier National Park or Pictured Rocks National Lakeshore, Michigan).

Beachcomber's Bonanza

Why not volunteer for a national park beach cleanup? Picking up trash will help make the beach safer for people and wildlife—and you might find something interesting!

Two artists have spent the last **10 years** collecting **trash** along the beaches of Point Reyes National Seashore in California and turning it into **works of art.**

Beachcombers search for treasure on the beach ... and sometimes they find trash too. Find and circle these items:

1. key
2. Statue of Liberty
3. crayon
4. tennis racket
5. 2 goldfish
6. 3 marbles
7. 4 balls
8. barrette
9. 2 bottle caps
10. photograph
11. car
12. compass
13. sunglasses
14. pearl
15. guitar pick
16. ring
17. beagle
18. 2 state names
19. kazoo
20. pink monster
21. shovel

105

STUMP
YOUR PARENTS

Many national parks are helping to save endangered and threatened species. Only a rare individual could answer all these questions—can your parents do it?

1 The endangered black-footed ferret has been reintroduced into Wind Cave National Park, after being nearly wiped out when people started eliminating its chief prey, the _____.
a. prairie dog
b. seagull
c. spotted salamander
d. tarantula

2 In the 1980s, there were just 22 California condors and all were in captivity. Since then, a program to breed and reintroduce condors has created a wild population of 400. You might see condors flying free in which of these parks?
a. Grand Canyon
b. Bryce Canyon
c. Zion
d. all of the above

3 True or false?
More than 99 percent of the species that have ever existed are now extinct.

4 Which of these endangered species can be found in Biscayne National Park?
a. Eastern indigo snake
b. Schaus's swallowtail butterfly
c. hawksbill sea turtle
d. all of the above

5 The endangered island fox lives only on:
a. the Channel Islands
b. the Fox Channel
c. the Venice Beach boardwalk
d. high mountaintops

6 Which park gives its name to a species of marmot, torrent salamander, mudminnow, pocket gopher, and grasshopper?
a. Capitol Reef National Park
b. Olympic National Park
c. Hot Springs National Park
d. Mammoth Cave National Park

7 True or false?
Wolves migrated to Michigan's Isle Royale National Park by walking 14 miles (23 km) across frozen Lake Superior.

8 The endangered northern spotted owl lives in which of these national parks?
a. Acadia
b. Glacier
c. Redwood
d. Great Smoky Mountains

9 In 1995, after wolves had become nearly extinct in the lower 48 states, biologists reintroduced them into Yellowstone National Park. How many wolves live in Yellowstone now?
a about 24
b. about 100
c. exactly 1,698
d. none

CHECK YOUR ANSWERS ON PAGE 153.

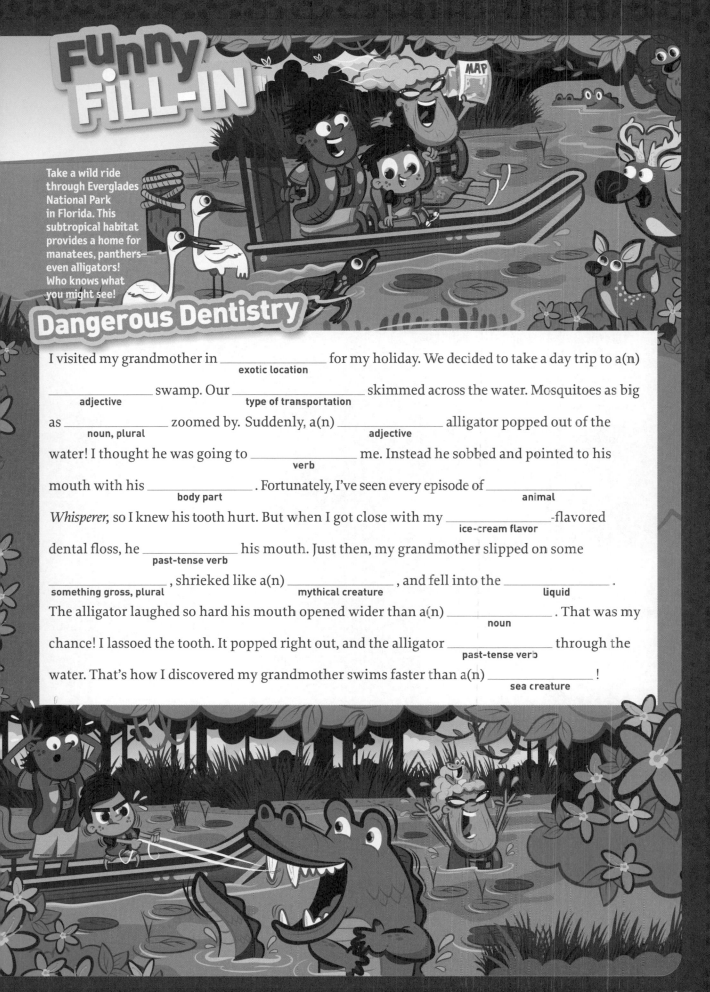

Funny Fill-In

Take a wild ride through Everglades National Park in Florida. This subtropical habitat provides a home for manatees, panthers—even alligators! Who knows what you might see!

Dangerous Dentistry

I visited my grandmother in _____ for my holiday. We decided to take a day trip to a(n)
_____ (exotic location)

_____ swamp. Our _____ skimmed across the water. Mosquitoes as big
(adjective)   (type of transportation)

as _____ zoomed by. Suddenly, a(n) _____ alligator popped out of the
   (noun, plural)   (adjective)

water! I thought he was going to _____ me. Instead he sobbed and pointed to his
         (verb)

mouth with his _____. Fortunately, I've seen every episode of _____
   (body part)   (animal)

Whisperer, so I knew his tooth hurt. But when I got close with my _____-flavored
              (ice-cream flavor)

dental floss, he _____ his mouth. Just then, my grandmother slipped on some
   (past-tense verb)

_____, shrieked like a(n) _____, and fell into the _____.
(something gross, plural)   (mythical creature)   (liquid)

The alligator laughed so hard his mouth opened wider than a(n) _____. That was my
                   (noun)

chance! I lassoed the tooth. It popped right out, and the alligator _____ through the
                  (past-tense verb)

water. That's how I discovered my grandmother swims faster than a(n) _____!
                  (sea creature)

COOL CAVES

1 On average, how long does it take for most caves to get big enough for a person to fit inside?
a. about 10 years
b. about 100 years
c. about 1,000 years
d. about 100,000 years

Explore Carlsbad Caverns (New Mexico), Mammoth Cave (Kentucky), or Wind Cave (South Dakota) for some underground adventure! But first, check out your cave comprehension here.

2 These icicle-shaped formations form as water drips from the cave ceiling. What are they called?
a. stalagmites
b. stalactites
c. icicles
d. rocks

3 These pointy formations grow up from the floor where water drops fall. What are they called?
a. stalagmites
b. stalactites
c. totems
d. chopsticks

4 True or false? All bats sleep in caves.

5 Until 1986, miners took what animal with them into caves to test if the air was breathable?
a. dogs
b. cats
c. snakes
d. canaries

6 Which of these creatures often lives in caves?
a. glowworm
b. ostrich
c. cow
d. elephant

7 When stalactites and stalagmites touch, they can form what kind of structure?
a. a column
b. a big rock
c. a waterfall
d. an ice pillar

8 Which national park holds the world's longest cave?
a. Mammoth Cave
b. Carlsbad Caverns
c. Wind Cave
d. Capitol Reef

Stalagmites and stalagtites in Carlsbad Caverns, New Mexico

9 Because there is no light, fish that live in caves are often _____.
a. blind
b. deaf
c. small
d. hungry

10 What do you call a person who studies caves?
a. a caveologist
b. a speleologist
c. an entomologist
d. a rock-and-roller

11 Carlsbad Cavern is home to hundreds of thousands of:
a. dragons
b. spelunkers
c. superheroes
d. bats

12 What is the name of these hollow tubes that grow from cave ceilings? Hint: The answer might make you thirsty.
a. soda straws
b. fire poles
c. hollow bats
d. bean poles

13 What 4,000-year-old treat was found in a cave in New Mexico?
a. a Twinkie
b. popcorn
c. Lucky Charms
d. graham crackers

14 The act of exploring caves is called _____.
a. hiding
b. diving
c. hiking
d. spelunking

109

CHECK YOUR ANSWERS ON PAGE 153.

Presidential Parks

United States presidents have worked and played in the national parks; presidents have helped to create the parks; and there are parks that honor presidents. Test your presidential park proficiency with these questions.

1 Who worked as a Yellowstone park ranger before becoming president?

- A. George Washington
- B. Grover Cleveland
- C. Theodore Roosevelt
- D. Gerald Ford

YELLOWSTONE NATIONAL PARK, Wyoming, Montana, and Idaho

2 In 1885, when the Washington Monument honoring George Washington was dedicated, it was the tallest building in the world. In 1889, which new structure surpassed this monument in height?

- A. the Sears Tower
- B. the White House
- C. the Eiffel tower
- D. none of the above

3 The Adams National Historical Park in Quincy, Massachusetts, preserves the birthplaces and homes of:

- A. John Adams (the second president)
- B. Morticia Addams
- C. John Quincy Adams (the sixth president)
- D. A and C

ADAMS NATIONAL HISTORICAL PARK, Massachusetts

WASHINGTON MONUMENT, Washington, D.C.

4 A large herd of Roosevelt elk lives in Olympic National Park, Washington. Who were these elk named after?

A. Franklin Delano Roosevelt
B. Eleanor Roosevelt
C. Theodore Roosevelt
D. Moose Roosevelt

OLYMPIC NATIONAL PARK, Washington

5 In the midst of the Civil War, before Yellowstone became the first national park, Abraham Lincoln signed a bill protecting which area for the enjoyment of the public?

A. National Mall
B. Gettysburg
C. Zion
D. Yosemite Valley

6 Where are the words of President Dwight D. Eisenhower inscribed?

A. Dinosaur National Monument
B. World War II Memorial
C. Devil's Golf Course, Death Valley
D. Capitol Reef National Park

7 In February 2015, President Obama announced that the National Park Service would be giving free admission to the national parks for a year to all_____.

A. veterinarians
B. rangers
C. fourth graders and their families
D. dogs and cats

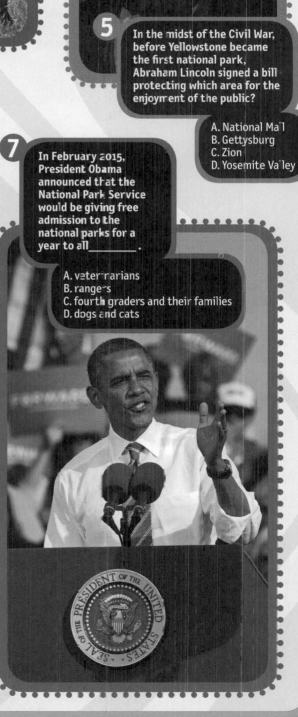

8 A national forest named for Lewis and Clark—here with guide Sacagawea—adjoins which national park?

A. Glacier
B. North Cascades
C. Hot Springs
D. Saguaro

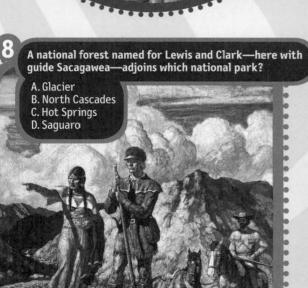

5 explosive facts about volcanoes

You can find volcanoes in several national parks—even active volcanoes! Read on for some wild facts about them.

1 Kilauea, in Hawai'i Volcanoes National Park, has been **erupting** continuously since **1983.**

2 Oregon's Crater Lake was formed when rain and snowmelt filled the **caldera**—or giant pit—left by a massive **volcanic** eruption.

3 About **1,000** years ago, a volcanic **eruption** formed the red-tinged **cinder cone** standing today at Sunset Crater Volcano National Monument, Arizona.

4 Lassen Volcanic National Park, California, has all of the four types of **volcanoes** found in the world— shield, plug dome, cinder cone, and composite.

5 The word **"volcano"** comes from the name of the Roman fire god, **Vulcan.**

Name That AMPHIBIAN

The presence of many amphibians in a national park shows the habitat is healthy and free from pollution. Can you identify these amphibians?

A Small, with dry, warty skin, at night it produces a high-pitched musical sound. It lives in parks in the Southwest, often hiding among rocks.

B Preferring to hide out under rocks and inside hollow logs, this creature found in the eastern United States and Canada is hard to spot!

Slinky salamanders

There are at least 30 species of salamanders in Great Smoky Mountains National Park.

C Its calls have been used as background nighttime sounds in old Hollywood movies. Despite its name, it lives mostly on the ground in parks in Washington and Oregon.

D You can name this endangered hopper, found in Pinnacles and other California parks, by looking at the color of its belly and legs.

113

CHECK YOUR ANSWERS ON PAGE 154.

Just Joking

Orcas live in groups called pods. They can be seen in the icy waters of Kenai Fjords National Park, Alaska.

KNOCK, KNOCK.

Who's there?
Walnut.
Walnut who?
I walnut leave without you.

TONGUE TWISTER!

Say this fast three times:

Selfish shellfish

What kind of **dinosaur** **Q** loves **English class?**

A thesaurus. **A**

HAHAHA!

You've **got** to be joking...

Q What do you say to a **rodent** when it leaves for **work?**

Have a mice day. **A**

JIM: What kind of whale flies?
NANCY: A pilot whale!

What in the World?

THE PARK AFTER DARK

What might you see in the national parks after sunset? Unscramble the labels to identify the after-dark scenes in these zoomed-in photos.

INGSPR EEERPP GOFR

_____

UNEQE FO HET HTNIG

_____

YLKMI AYW

_____

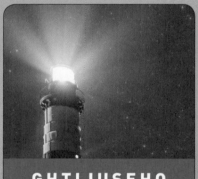

GHTLIUSEHO

_____

ITLETL NRBOW TBA

_____

LYFIRFE

_____

LFUL OMON

_____

ORRAAU RELIBOAS

_____

WKHA TMHO

_____

CHECK YOUR ANSWERS ON PAGE 154.

Funny FILL-IN

During the chilly winter, head to the slopes! Rocky Mountain National Park is the perfect place to explore in the snow. Some winter wildlife is easy to spot, while others put on snow-white disguises, becoming almost invisible. So look close and get ready to uncover an amazing winter wonderland.

Fun Fact! In summer, a ptarmigan's feathers are brown and white to blend in with rocks; in winter they are white to blend in with the snow.

Rocky Mountain National Park

Today, we're way up in the mountains of Rocky Mountain National Park in Colorado. We're surrounded by snow as deep as my _____ !
                                                                                                                              body part

We're just about to strap on our snow-_____ and go for a walk when we see a
                                          clothing item, plural

large _____ poking out of the snow. I'd recognize _____ like that
        body part   *same body part, plural*

anywhere—a snowshoe hare. It _____ away, and we follow it _____
                              verb ending in –s   *adverb ending in –ly*

until we come to a clearing. Wow! Whoever was here before us made some really _____
                                                                               adjective

snow sculptures. There is a hare, a pika, an elk, and even a(n) _____—all made
                                                                type of animal

of snow! I decide to make a snow _____ with a really _____ nose.
                                  your name   *adjective*

_____ makes one with a great big _____ . But I think first prize should
friend's name   *body part*

go to a white-tailed ptarmigan—until it suddenly _____ away!
                                                  verb ending in –s

Redwood Roundup

These hikers are trekking around towering trees in Redwood National Park in California. Join the fun by finding the 15 items below.

1. banana slug
2. skunk
3. binoculars
4. yellow raincoat
5. Roosevelt elk
6. porcupine
7. sunglasses
8. blue tent
9. park ranger
10. red backpack
11. trekking poles
12. toy airplane
13. lantern
14. frogs
15. map

HISTORIC TRAILS

Hop into history! National historic trails trace important journeys of the past. On these historic routes you can hike, drive, boat, and visit historic exhibits. Show what you know about what happened along these routes, then match each trail to its correct location on the map.

1 PONY EXPRESS

The Pony Express riders of the Old West delivered mail from St. Joseph, Missouri, to Sacramento, California—1,800 miles (2,897 km)—in _____ .
a. 10 days
b. 3 weeks
c. 2 months
d. automobiles

2 SELMA TO MONTGOMERY

For five days in 1965, marchers walked this 54-mile (87-km) route along the highway during a historic march for _____ .
a. health care
b. voting rights
c. climate change
d. exercise

3 LEWIS AND CLARK

Although we don't know the exact route of the famous transcontinental expedition of 1804–1806, at one point on the trail you can see _____ .
a. William Clark's signature carved into rock
b. Sacagawea's diary
c. Lewis's leftover dinner
d. the group's empty soda cans

4 IDITAROD

Teams of mushers with dogsleds carried life-saving serum over the snow and ice to Nome, Alaska, on part of this route—674 miles (1,085 km) in five and a half days—during a 1925 outbreak of _____ .

a. cabin fever　　**c.** diphtheria
b. chicken pox　　**d.** ebola

5 CAPTAIN JOHN SMITH

America's first national historic trail on the water is a series of boating routes along the Chesapeake Bay and its tributaries, generally following the 1607–1609 explorations of Captain John Smith. Who is remembered for saving Smith's life?

a. Superman
b. Pocahontas
c. Sacagawea
d. Elsa

6 MORMON PIONEERS

This trail from Nauvoo, Illinois, to Salt Lake City, Utah, traces the migration of the 19th-century Mormons who headed west seeking religious freedom. Along the route you can see:

a. old wagon ruts
b. icebergs
c. manatees
d. polar bears

7 TRAIL OF TEARS

This historic trail traces two routes taken by the Cherokee people who were forced to relocate from their homes in Georgia, Alabama, and Tennessee to live in "Indian Territory" (now Oklahoma). In 1838–1839, about how many Cherokees moved?

a. 500
b. 5,000
c. 15,000
d. 15,000,000

8–14 MATCH EACH OF THESE
PLACES TO THE RED MARKER THAT SHOWS ITS CORRECT LOCATION ON THE MAP.

Name That CAMPSITE CRITTER

When you're in the national parks, animals big and small are all around! You may see creatures scramble or crawl at your picnic spot, on the hiking trail, or even in your campground. Take this quiz to see if you can identify some cool common critters in the parks.

A This bushy-tailed visitor to park campgrounds will eat almost anything. If it's not raiding picnic baskets or garbage cans, look for it near the water, where it feeds on frogs, fish, clams, and crayfish.

B This skinny, striped reptile is about as long as a baseball bat. It isn't venomous, but it may bite if you pick it up. It is common in parks except in the dry southwest.

D Look for this common reptile near trees, especially in south-eastern parks such as Shenandoah. It's often seen soaking up the sun on logs, rocks, or fences.

C This cute critter often begs for food from people in Grand Canyon and other western parks.

Do not feed

Keep wildlife wild! You may see signs in many national parks reminding visitors that "handouts harm." Animals fed by people learn to raid picnic tables, backpacks, tents, and garbage cans—behavior that can be unsafe for animals and park visitors.

CHECK YOUR ANSWERS ON PAGE 154.

RANGER TIPS

TOP FIVE URBAN ESCAPES

1. Gateway National Recreation Area, New York/New Jersey
2. Golden Gate National Recreation Area, California
3. Rock Creek Park, Washington, D.C.
4. Santa Monica Mountains National Recreation Area, California
5. Cuyahoga Valley National Park, Ohio

Want to know which national parks top the list? Every park is amazing, but here are some suggestions for a variety of great parks to visit and for wildlife activities you can do, too!

TOP FIVE NATIONAL PARKS FOR CAMPING

1. Yosemite
2. Yellowstone
3. Lake Mead National Recreation Area
4. Grand Canyon
5. Great Smoky Mountains

FIVE FUN WAYS TO OBSERVE NATURE

1. Look for shapes in the clouds.
2. Watch ants and see what they're doing.
3. Try to identify bird calls.
4. Take photographs of animals.
5. Look at tree bark with a magnifying glass.

TOP FIVE NATIONAL PARK HIKES

1. Endless Wall Trail—New River Gorge National River
2. Cadillac Mountain—Acadia National Park
3. Kīlauea Iki Trail—Hawaiʻi Volcanoes National Park
4. Hoh River Trail—Olympic National Park
5. Ramsey Cascades—Great Smoky Mountains National Park

Undersea Stars

Do marine musicians play air guitar in the undersea wilderness of Biscayne National Park? Probably not, but there are some fishy instruments hidden in this picture. Can you spot the 10 musical instruments listed here?

1. piano
2. drums
3. flute
4. saxophone
5. triangle
6. violin
7. accordion
8. guitar
9. maracas
10. tambourine

Many animals living in the waters of **Biscayne** National Park resemble **plants**—for example, **sea cucumbers**, sponges, and **coral**.

CHECK YOUR ANSWERS ON PAGE 154.

STUMP YOUR PARENTS

Many national parks commemorate important women in U.S. history. How much do you (or your parents) know about these memorable women?

1 Clara Barton National Historic Site in Maryland honors the woman who founded the _____.
a. Girl Scouts
b. San Francisco Ballet
c. American Red Cross
d. Cleveland Nursing School

2 At Lewis and Clark National Historical Park in Oregon, there's a statue of the guide Sacagawea showing her carrying _____.

a. her infant son
b. a large backpack
c. a frying pan
d. a bow and arrows

3 In Yellowstone, in 1918, Claire Marie Hodges was the first woman to _____.
a. visit every national park
b. work as a national park ranger
c. paint Yellowstone Falls
d. discover a new geyser

4 The Maggie L. Walker National Historic Site in Virginia honors the woman who in 1903 became the first female African–American _____.
a. senator
b. college professor
c. dentist
d. bank president

5 At which national historic site can you see items that members of the National Woman's Party wore as they paraded for women's right to vote?
a. Tuskegee Institute (Alabama)
b. Chimney Rock (Nebraska)
c. Grant-Kohrs Ranch (Montana)
d. Sewall-Belmont House and Museum (Washington, D.C.)

6 In what year were female rangers in the national parks first permitted to wear the same "Smokey Bear" hats as male park rangers?
a. 1918
b. 1950
c. 1962
d. 1978

7 Eleanor Roosevelt National Historic Site in New York is named for this tireless advocate for human rights, equality for women, and world peace. She was called the _____.
a. "First Lady of the World"
b. "Lady With the Lamp"
c. "Angel of the Battlefield"
d. "Woman Who Lived With Gorillas"

8 Rosie the Riveter/World War II Home Front National Historical Park in California commemorates the war effort of millions of women in the 1940s who worked _____.
a. making weapons
b. building ships
c. driving trucks
d. all of the above

We Can Do It!

CHECK YOUR ANSWERS ON PAGE 154.

Watery WONDERS

Congaree
National Park

How's the water? In many national parks you'll want to jump in and cool off—in the sea, bay, lake, creek, or brook. But first, get your feet wet with these H_2O questions.

1 On the vast floodplain of Congaree National Park, South Carolina, there are many lakes that formed when a river changed its course and left a former bend in the river cut off from the water's flow. These are called _____ .

a. oxbow lakes
b. finger lakes
c. crater lakes
d. bays

2 Bear Lake, in Rocky Mountain National Park, is one of the few high-mountain lakes in Colorado visitors can reach by _____ .

a. jet plane
b. water skis
c. paved road
d. water slide

3 To avoid being trapped against the rocks when the tide rolls in, before hiking along the beaches of Olympic National Park you should check the _____ .

a. temperature
b. tide schedule
c. ozone level
d. sea otter population

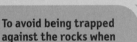

National Park of
American Samoa

Olympic National Park

4 The Grand Canyon was formed by _____ .

a. moles and other digging animals
b. a giant earthquake in 1492
c. dinosaurs
d. erosion by the Colorado River

5 National Park of American Samoa features coral reefs where visitors can go _____ .

a. white-water rafting
b. hunting for walrus
c. snorkeling
d. all of the above

Acadia
National Park

6 Most of Acadia National Park is located on _____.

a. New Hampshire's coast
b. Mount Desert Island, Maine
c. Lake Acadia, Vermont
d. Acadia Canyon

7 Which national park is sometimes called the "Galápagos of North America" because of the large number of species that live only on or near those islands?

a. Boston Harbor Islands, Massachusetts
b. Gulf Islands, Florida
c. Apostle Islands, Wisconsin
d. Channel Islands, California

8 Water features known as fjords that give Kenai Fjords National Park its name are best described as _____.

a. deep inlets of the sea
b. finger lakes
c. waterfalls
d. river deltas

Isle Royale
National Park

9 At which national park can visitors soak in waters that have been heated deep under the ground?

a. Gates of the Arctic, Alaska
b. Big Bend, Texas
c. Hot Springs, Arkansas
d. Death Valley, California

10 For many years, at the remote and wild Isle Royale National Park on Lake Superior (Michigan), biologists have studied the predator–prey interactions between

_____.

a. grizzlies and coyotes
b. gray wolves and moose
c. yellow-bellied sapsuckers and red squirrels
d. none of the above

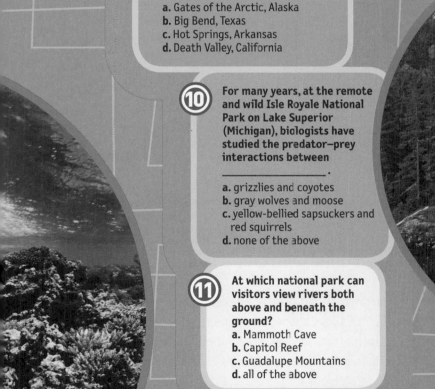

11 At which national park can visitors view rivers both above and beneath the ground?

a. Mammoth Cave
b. Capitol Reef
c. Guadalupe Mountains
d. all of the above

CHECK YOUR ANSWERS ON PAGE 155.

RANGER TIPS

For year-round fun, try these Junior Ranger ideas for outdoor projects, or come up with your own!

PRESSING LEAVES IN THE FALL

Press colorful leaves to save them.

1. With an adult to help, place a leaf between two pieces of wax paper.
2. Put a thin towel over the wax paper on an ironing board.
3. Press with a warm iron for two to five minutes; turn paper and leaf over.
4. Press on the other side for another two to five minutes.
5. Cut around the leaf, leaving a bit of wax paper to seal it.

BIRD FEED FOR WINTER

Make a tasty treat for birds!

1. Cut a "doughnut" shape out of cardboard.
2. Spread peanut butter on it, and then sprinkle birdseed or popcorn over that.
3. Use string or yarn to tie it to a tree outside.
4. Wait to see what birds (or other small critters) find it.

PONDING IN SPRING

Ponder the pond!
Look in the water. Do you see masses of eggs left by frogs or salamanders? Newly hatched tadpoles? What about swimming insects? Try to visit the same pond in a few days to see what changes have occurred.

BIRD-WATCHING IN SUMMER

Go bird-watching! Here are details you'll need to record:

- The bird's size, shape, color, and feather markings
- Is the bird soaring like an eagle? Hammering on a tree with its beak, like a woodpecker? What is special about it?
- What habitat is it in—water, forest, meadow, seashore?
- Song: Listen for the bird's call. Each species sings a unique song.

Later you can check a guidebook to identify the bird based on your field observations.

Funny Fill-IN

If you trek up to one of Yosemite's waterfalls, be prepared to get soaked! The wind can blow water right onto the trail. For a drier diversion, find a forest path and look for rabbits, coyotes, or mule deer. No matter which path you choose, there's always lots to see in this national park!

Fun Fact! Bridalveil Fall in Yosemite National Park got its name because when the wind blows, the water blows sideways, resembling a bride's veil.

Yosemite Yuk-Yuks

In Yosemite, we _____ close behind the park ranger
                        verb

until we come to an area where there are _____ rock cliffs that are _____
                                          adjective   number

times taller than the _____ at home. We hear _____ roaring
                      type of building, plural   adjective

and smashing sounds. It's Yosemite Falls, the _____ waterfall in the country!
                                              adjective ending in –est

"Oh, good! My friends are here," says the park ranger. We start _____ over to ask
                                                                verb ending in –ing

some _____-looking people sitting on _____ outside a lodge, but instead
     adjective   noun, plural

the park ranger stops very _____ . In front of us _____ on the grass
                           adverb ending in –ly   verb ending in –ing

are _____ mule deer. They have ears like a(n) _____ . "Shhh," whispers the
    number   type of animal

park ranger, and he starts moving his ears up and down. Then one of the mule deer moves

its ears, too! The park ranger nods in thanks and _____ over to a fallen log. Inside
                                                  verb ending in –s

we find _____ _____ squirrels, and they have hidden some nuts inside!
        number   color

National Mall, WASHINGTON, D.C.

You could spend days (and nights) exploring the sites—indoors and out—at the National Mall in Washington, D.C. How much do you know about the nation's capital? Take this quiz and see if you're a Capital Insider!

1 The National Mall extends 2 miles (3.2 km) west from the steps of the U.S. Capitol to _____ .
a. West Virginia
b. the Pacific Ocean
c. the Lincoln Memorial
d. Pacific Avenue

2 The National Mall has been the site of _____ .
a. protest marches
b. music concerts
c. fireworks shows
d. all of the above

3 Which of the following is NOT on the National Mall?
a. Ford's Theater
b. National Museum of African Art
c. National Museum of the American Indian
d. Korean War Veterans Memorial

4 How many U.S. flags encircle the base of the Washington Monument?
a. 50—one for each state
b. 896—one for each step going to the top
c. 14—13 for the colonies plus one for luck
d. 10—one for each letter in "Washington"

5 The Franklin Delano Roosevelt Memorial includes a sculpture of FDR in a_____ .
a. battleship   c. wheelchair
b. swimsuit   d. bathtub

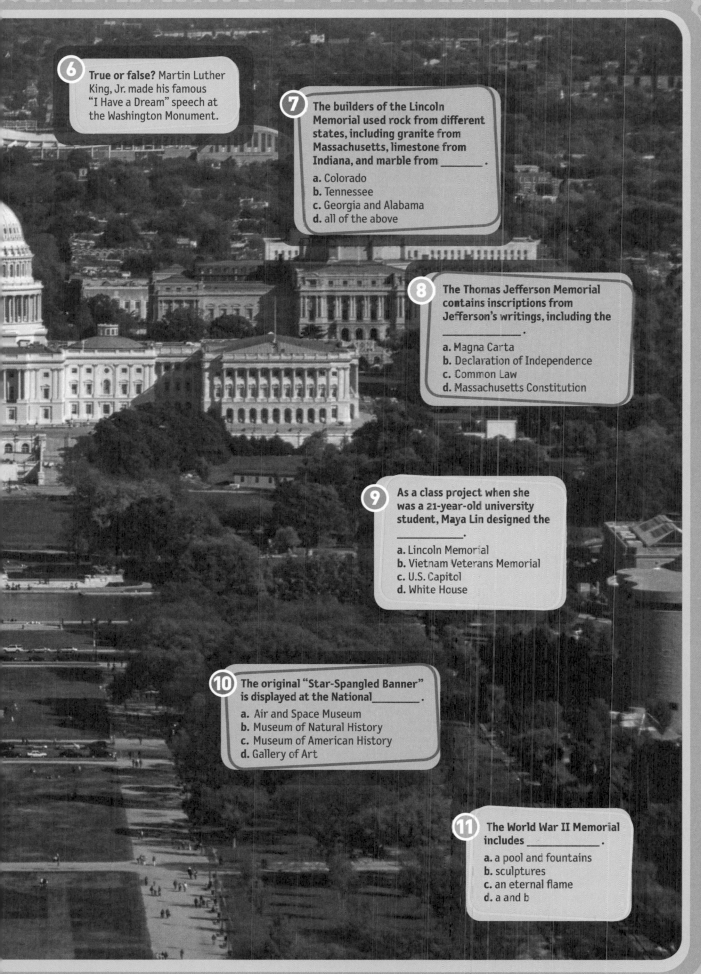

6 **True or false?** Martin Luther King, Jr. made his famous "I Have a Dream" speech at the Washington Monument.

7 The builders of the Lincoln Memorial used rock from different states, including granite from Massachusetts, limestone from Indiana, and marble from _____ .

a. Colorado
b. Tennessee
c. Georgia and Alabama
d. all of the above

8 The Thomas Jefferson Memorial contains inscriptions from Jefferson's writings, including the _____ .

a. Magna Carta
b. Declaration of Independence
c. Common Law
d. Massachusetts Constitution

9 As a class project when she was a 21-year-old university student, Maya Lin designed the _____ .

a. Lincoln Memorial
b. Vietnam Veterans Memorial
c. U.S. Capitol
d. White House

10 The original "Star-Spangled Banner" is displayed at the National_____ .

a. Air and Space Museum
b. Museum of Natural History
c. Museum of American History
d. Gallery of Art

11 The World War II Memorial includes _____ .

a. a pool and fountains
b. sculptures
c. an eternal flame
d. a and b

The River Wild

Steer this raft safely from the LAUNCH to the TAKE-OUT site. Only one route offers thrills and avoids spills and chills.

Rafters in **Big Bend** National Park (Texas) can float down the **Rio Grande River** enclosed by **sheer cliffs** on both sides.

LAUNCH

TAKE-OUT

What in the World?

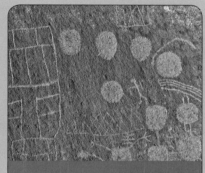

LFFIC NGELLDWI

_____

YPPROGETLH

_____

ADREM CHCATER

_____

ANCOE

_____

ERPOYTT

_____

ASIMOCCN

_____

WEJRYEL

_____

BLUEPO

_____

DARHEAROW

_____

Just Joking

Fewer than 100 Florida panthers are believed to live in the wild today.

KNOCK, KNOCK.

Who's there?
Tibia.
Tibia who?
It's going tibia good day!

JIM: How does a snail feel when it loses its shell?

NANCY: A little sluggish.

What does a **lizard** Q add when it remodels **its kitchen?**

Rep-tiles. A

TONGUE TWISTER!

Say this fast three times:

Six slim sycamore saplings

You've **got** to be joking...

Q What kind of **bird** is bad at **catching fish?**

A pelican't. A

TAKE A LOOK! YELLOWSTONE NATIONAL PARK

< FIND THESE **NATIONAL PARK** ANIMALS >

1 raccoon
4 bears
2 squirrels

7 animals with antlers
5 wolves
1 bald eagle

2 beavers
3 bison
2 foxes

Fun Fact!

Yellowstone National Park sits atop a massive **supervolcano** that last erupted **640,000** years ago.

133

CHECK YOUR ANSWERS ON PAGE 155.

STUMP
YOUR PARENTS

Within and beyond the 50 states, some national parks have an international flavor. Quiz your family on their international park IQ!

1 Sitka National Historical Park, Alaska, marks the site of an 1804 battle between native Tlingits and military forces and fur traders from _____ .
a. France
b. England
c. China
d. Russia

2 In 1542, Juan Rodriguez Cabrillo became the first European to land on what is now the west coast of California. Cabrillo National Monument marks the spot, in the city of
_____ .
a. San Diego
b. San Francisco
c. Las Vegas
d. Miami

3 The Golden Spike National Historic Site in Utah remembers the legacy of the more than 11,000 Chinese workers who came to the United States to build the _____ .
a. Great Wall
b. telegraph
c. Internet
d. Transcontinental Railroad

4 The only way to drive to Roosevelt Campobello International Park is across a bridge from Maine—and an international border. The park is administered jointly by the United States and which other country?
a. Mexico
b. Canada
c. Cuba
d. Italy

5 On St. Croix in the U.S. Virgin Islands, Christiansted National Historic Site preserves historic buildings from the period when the island belonged to _____ .
a. Spain
b. Belgium
c. Denmark
d. England

6 True or false?
Jean Lafitte National Historical Park and Preserve, which honors the Acadian (Cajun) people who settled in southern Louisiana in the 18th century, was named for a notorious pirate.

7 San Juan Island National Historical Park in Washington State marks the site of a territorial dispute of 1859 in which Britain sent warships here after an American farmer shot a British company's _____ .
a. pig
b. horse
c. falcon
d. turkey

8 On the Pacific island of Saipan, American Memorial Park honors those who died in the 1944 Battle of _____ .
a. the Bulge
b. Saipan
c. Bull Run
d. Alamo

9 On New York's Ellis Island, 12 million immigrants were processed before entering the United States. When the station opened in 1892, 17-year-old Annie Moore was the first to pass through. Annie came from _____ .
a. England
b. Germany
c. Ireland
d. Italy

CHECK YOUR ANSWERS ON PAGE 155.

Find the HIDDEN ANIMALS

Animals often blend into their environments for protection. Find each animal listed below in one of the pictures. Write the letter of the correct picture next to each animal's name.

1. spider _____
2. stick insect _____
3. horned lizard _____
4. frogfish _____

CHECK YOUR ANSWERS ON PAGE 155.

Funny Fill-In

You can never predict what the volcanoes will do next at Hawai'i Volcanoes National Park. Look for ancient petroglyphs or walk through a lava tube in the rain forest—as long as fresh lava isn't blocking the path!

Fun Fact! Kilauea is the world's most active volcano. It produces so much lava, it's added about 500 acres (202 ha) of new land to the Big Island since 1983!

Lovin' Lava

At Hawai'i Volcanoes National Park, we look out over a crater as big as

a(n) _____ with _____ dried lava everywhere. _____ clouds of steam
　　　　noun　　　　　　　　color　　　　　　　　　　　　adjective

seep up from belowground. We _____ down a path with _____ ferns growing
　　　　　　　　　　　　　　　　verb　　　　　　　　　　　　color

on either side. This place looks like a prehistoric jungle—I wonder if a(n) _____
　　　　　　　　　　　　　　　　　　　　　　　　　　　　　　　　type of dinosaur

will appear! Then, suddenly, the sky darkens and it starts to pour down _____ .
　　　　　　　　　　　　　　　　　　　　　　　　　　　　　　　　type of liquid

"_____ for it!" the ranger shouts, and we all take off down the path to the _____
　　verb　　　　　　　　　　　　　　　　　　　　　　　　　　　　　　　　　body part

of a cave. When we step inside, we see the _____ thing ever: The walls are
　　　　　　　　　　　　　　　　　adjective ending in –est

coated with _____ lava! The ranger tells us that this is a lava tube. It was made when
　　　　　color

_____ lava flowed underneath Earth's surface. We hear a loud _____ from
　adjective　　　　　　　　　　　　　　　　　　　　　　　　　　　　noise

outside the lava tube. Was that thunder, or a volcanic eruption? Or maybe even a herd of

dinosaurs running past?

5 mighty facts about bison

The American bison has recovered from the brink of extinction. You can see herds in western parks such as Yellowstone and Grand Teton (Wyoming).

1 The **bison** is the largest **land mammal** in North America.

2 In **winter,** a bison's fur is so **thick** and well insulated that **snow** collects on its back without **melting!**

3 Bison have **good hearing** and a keen sense of smell—but poor **eyesight.**

4 The herd of about **5,000 bison** in Yellowstone National Park is the largest **wild** population.

5 **Bison** can run **30 miles** an hour (48 km/h).

What in the World?

ANIMAL FEET

Feet help us get where we need to go. An animal's feet may be adapted for grasping prey, hopping over winter snow, or skittering across a rock. Unscramble the letters to identify just whose feet these are.

DGBAER

_____

LEGEA

_____

MANAALSDER

_____

NNRRDREUOA

_____

EOWSNSHO AHRE

_____

ACRCONO

_____

YFL

_____

ROELBST

_____

INUNTMOA TGAO

_____

Awesome park animals

Here are a few surprising facts about some less common animals found in national parks and preserves.

A sea otter has **1,000,000** hairs on a **POSTAGE-STAMP-SIZE** area of its body.

A baby **HUMPBACK WHALE** drinks up to three **BATHTUBFULS OF MILK** each day.

MOM, I'M REALLY THIRSTY!

A **FLAMINGO** CAN EAT ONLY WHEN **ITS HEAD** IS UPSIDE DOWN.

Seagulls **sometimes** sit on **PELICANS'** **heads.**

National Parks

TRIVIA CHALLENGE

Discovery! Technology! Innovation! The very idea of national parks could be called an American invention. The United States was the first country to pass laws that set aside natural areas for public enjoyment. Can you discover the answers to these questions about national parks that honor innovators and inventors?

1 The Benjamin Franklin National Memorial in Philadelphia offers exhibits on Franklin's life and his many inventions. Franklin's face is on today's _____.

BENJAMIN FRANKLIN NATIONAL MEMORIAL, Pennsylvania

A. $20 bill
B. $100 bill
C. $500 bill
D. dime

2 The Thomas Edison National Historical Park, New Jersey, preserves the laboratory of the inventor who holds the record for the highest number of patents ever received by one person. How many patents did Edison get?

A. 59
B. 599
C. 1,093
D. too many to count

THOMAS EDISON NATIONAL HISTORICAL PARK, New Jersey

3 At Steamtown National Historic Site, Pennsylvania, some visitors _____.

A. ride a steam-powered train
B. see the roundhouse where trains are maintained
C. view a 1903 steam engine
D. all of the above

STEAMTOWN NATIONAL HISTORIC SITE, Pennsylvania

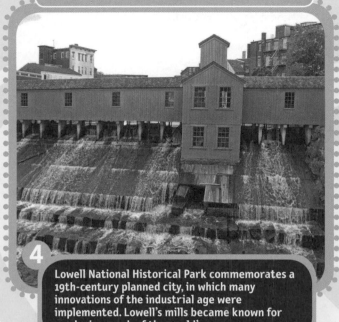

4

Lowell National Historical Park commemorates a 19th-century planned city, in which many innovations of the industrial age were implemented. Lowell's mills became known for producing much of the world's _____ .

A. corn meal
B. water
C. lumber
D. cloth

5

In the 1850s, the world's largest steam-driven mining hoist raised and lowered equipment through the shaft at Quincy Mine, which is now part of this park. The mine produced _____ .

A. gold
B. diamonds
C. copper
D. lumber

6

The Wright Brothers National Memorial, on the Outer Banks of North Carolina, is the site of the first _____ .

A. powered flight
B. airplane speed race
C. aerial battle
D. jet-plane flight

7

True or false? The telephone invented by Alexander Graham Bell is displayed at the National Air and Space Museum, Washington, D.C.

Bell (left) shows his assistant, Watson, his telephone device.

CHECK YOUR ANSWERS ON PAGE 156.

DOG DAZE

Rock Creek Park in Washington, D.C., is the largest **urban park** in the national park system. **Dogs** (on leash) can be taken on **wooded** trails in the park.

The eight snapshots above were taken at this dog park. Find the scene that appears in each picture.
Hint: Some of the snapshots are upside down or sideways.

CHECK YOUR ANSWERS ON PAGE 156.

Funny Fill-IN

Get to the bottom of the Grand Canyon! Two great ways to get the lowdown on this great gorge are rafting on the Colorado River and riding a mule down the steep trail along the canyon walls. Get ready to explore this amazing canyon!

Fun Fact! The Grand Canyon's California condor is the largest land bird in North America, with a wingspan of nine feet (2.7 m).

Grand Canyon National Park

White-water rafting in Grand Canyon National Park is

more fun than _____ and just a little less scary than _____
          your favorite sport   verb ending in –ing

in _____ wearing only a(n) _____ . I'm soaked, but it's
      name of a place   clothing item

_____ out and I feel _____ . When our raft is _____
   adjective   adjective   verb ending in –ed

into the air by a wave, I hear someone yell "_____ !" After rafting, we head to
                                                          silly word

_____ _____ Lodge. There, we meet _____ and _____ ,
   adjective   noun   girl's name   boy's name

the two mules taking us down into the canyon. But when we try to start out,

_____ sits down and won't move! We offer her a(n) _____ .
   same girl's name   type of vegetable

Nope. Then we offer her _____ , and she _____ ! We start to
                                  your favorite treat   verb ending in –s

_____ down the trail. The view is amazing. I try to take a selfie, but
   verb

_____ and his/her mule keep photobombing me!
   friend's name

MAP MANIA!
EXTREME PARKS

Wow! Have you reached the LAST PAGE? Here's a FINAL QUIZ to celebrate. Check out these questions about the oldest, longest, deepest, and other extremes in the national parks, then match each park to its map location.

1 GREAT BASIN

This park in Nevada has the southernmost _____ in North America:

a. sand
b. turtle
c. glacier
d. cactus

2 DEATH VALLEY

The lowest point in the United States—282 feet (86 m) below sea level—is in Death Valley, California, and is named _____.

a. Badwater Basin
b. Down Deep
c. Low Valley
d. So Low

3 HOT SPRINGS

Congress voted to protect this area in Arkansas, believed to contain healing springs, as a "reservation" in 1832, before Yellowstone. It is still the National Park Service's _____.

a. oldest unit
b. hottest unit
c. wildest unit
d. most visited unit

4 CONGAREE

This wild park, not far from Columbia, South Carolina, boasts the continent's largest remaining _____.

a. tree, a loblolly pine
b. southern old-growth bottomland forest
c. woolly mammoth
d. Viking ship

⑤ CRATER LAKE

Filling the huge pit created by a volcanic eruption, Crater Lake, Oregon, is the deepest lake in the United States. How deep is it?

a. 500 feet (152 m)
b. 1,248 feet (380 m)
c. 1,943 feet (592 m)
d. too deep to measure

⑥ MAMMOTH CAVE

More than 390 miles (628 km) of cave passages have been mapped here, making this Kentucky park home to the world's _____.

a. deepest cave
b. longest known cave
c. muddiest spelunkers
d. largest bats

⑦ ACADIA

At Acadia, Maine, the first eastern national park, many people climb Cadillac Mountain very early in the morning to be among the first in the country to see the _____.

a. sunrise
b. birds getting worms
c. manatees
d. morning news

8–14 MATCH EACH OF THESE
PLACES TO THE RED MARKER THAT SHOWS ITS CORRECT LOCATION ON THE MAP.

Wisconsin
Michigan
Illinois Indiana Ohio
ouri Kentucky
ansas Tennessee
Alabama Georgia
Mississippi
Louisiana Florida
CANADA
U.S.
Vermont New Hampshire
Maine B
Massachusetts
New York
Rhode Island
Connecticut
New Jersey
Pennsylvania
Delaware
Maryland
West Virginia
Virginia
North Carolina
South Carolina
ATLANTIC OCEAN
F
G

Alaska (U.S.)
U.S.
Hawai'i (U.S.)
PACIFIC OCEAN
Hawai'i

0   200 miles
0   200 kilometers

145

Answers

National Parks Road Trip! pages 10–11

1. **d**
2. **True.** The humpbacks spend winters near the islands of Hawaii, returning to Alaska as the weather warms.
3. **False.** Explorers gave the geyser this name because it erupts faithfully within every two hours. Its water is much too hot for a shower.
4. **d**
5. **a**
6. **a**
7. **a**
8. **c**
9. **True.**
10. **a**
11. **True.** People also used this large bucket to gather guano to make fertilizer. People rode in it until 1925, when a staircase was built into the cave.

What in the World? page 12

From top left, across rows:
**BIGHORN SHEEP, REDWOOD TREES, SEA OTTER
RED ROCK CRAB, CRATER LAKE, KELP FOREST
ORCA, MOUNT RAINIER, NORTHERN PYGMY OWL**

Find the Hidden Animals, page 17

1. **D**
2. **B**
3. **A**
4. **C**

Perfect Match, pages 18-19

Name That Wildflower, page 20

A. **saguaro cactus flower**
B. **glacier lily**
C. **mountain laurel**
D. **Haleakala silversword**

Stump Your Parents, page 21

1. **a**   4. **c**   7. **c**
2. **d**   5. **d**   8. **c**
3. **c**   6. **b**   9. **b**

What in the World? page 22

From top left, across rows:
**GOLDEN GATE BRIDGE, ALCATRAZ ISLAND,
    HANG GLIDER
RED-TAILED HAWK, BANANA SLUG, SEA LION
SUTRO BATHS, POPPIES, GRAY WHALE**

National Parks Trivia Challenge, pages 24-25

1. **B** (Joshua Tree National Park straddles the Mojave and Colorado deserts.)
2. **D**
3. **D**
4. **C**
5. **B** (The pronghorn—which is often mistaken for a small antelope—is the fastest land animal in the United States.)
6. **D**
7. **C**
8. **C**

Undersea Skiing, page 27

What in the World? page 28

From top left, across rows:
AIRBOAT, MULE, KAYAK
HIKING BOOTS, WHITE-WATER RAFT,
CROSS-COUNTRY SKIS
SNOWSHOES, FERRY, STEAM TRAIN

Name That Shell, page 29

A. **sand dollar**
B. **Florida fighting conch**
C. **cowrie**
D. **cockleshell**

Grand Canyon Adventure, pages 30-31

1. **d**
2. **True.** The canyon is made from sedimentary rocks deposited in layers by wind or water. The bottom layers were the first to be deposited; the top layers were the last.
3. **c**
4. **False.** Native American tribes, including the Hualapt, Havasupai, and Navajo, live on reservations in the Grand Canyon.
5. **a**   9. **d**
6. **c**   10. **b**
7. **d**   11. **d**
8. **c**
12. **True.** Some layers are made of sand, lime, or mud that hardened into rock.
13. **b**
14. **a**
15. **c**

Take a Look! Olympic National Park, page 33

Double Take, National Mall, page 34

Find the Hidden Animals, page 35

1. **C**
2. **D**
3. **A**
4. **B**

Take the Plunge, page 37

Map Mania! Park Explorer, pages 40-41

1. **b**
2. **a.** Mount McKinley, the tallest in North America, was officially renamed Denali—the name it was given by the Alaska Native people—in 2015.
3. **c**
4. **c**
5. **True.** The wind that gave the cave its name results from the difference in atmospheric pressure between the cave and the surface.
6. **False.** The islands are located in the Santa Barbara Channel, off the Southern California coast.
7. **b**
8. **Great Smoky Mountains: F**
9. **Grand Teton: A**
10. **Zion: E**
11. **Acadia: C**
12. **Wind Cave: B**
13. **Channel Islands: D**
14. **Gates of the Arctic: G**

Animal Jam, page 42

What in the World? page 43

From top left, across rows:
**SEA URCHIN, BARNACLES, SEA STAR
SEA ANEMONE, SEAWEED, HERMIT CRAB
LIMPET, JELLYFISH, LOBSTER**

Name That Bird, page 44

A. **northern cardinal**
B. **golden bellied grosbeak**
C. **rufous hummingbird**
D. **American goldfinch**

Stump Your Parents, page 45

1. **a**
2. **b**
3. **a**
4. **a**
5. **c**
6. **a**
7. **c**
8. **b**
9. **d**

Bark Park, page 47

Take a Look! Biscayne National Park, page 48

Mount Rushmore Math, pages 50-51

1. **c**
2. **b**
3. **c**
4. **c**
5. **a**
6. **b**
7. **True.** The faces are each 60 feet (18.3 m) high.
8. **a**
9. **b**
10. **False.** The project was started by sculptor

Korczak Ziolkowski in 1984 and his family still continues to work on it.

11. **b**
12. **c**
13. **b**
14. **b**
15. **c**

Up, Up, and Away, page 52

What in the World? page 53

From top left, across rows:
BISON, QUAIL, MOOSE
MULE DEER, PRONGHORN, HORNED LIZARD
WOODPECKER, DALL SHEEP, STAG BEETLE

Stump Your Parents, page 55

1. **a**
2. **c**
3. **d**
4. **True.** Male mosquitos live off juices from plants and decaying material.
5. **False.** In most frog species, the females are larger.
6. **d**
7. **a**
8. **True.** Male barn swallows try to attract females by displaying their tails, and females seem to prefer males with long tails that are equal lengths on each side.
9. **b**

Name That Insect, page 57

A. **odorous house ants**
B. **monarch butterflies**
C. **grasshopper**
D. **fireflies**

Map Mania! Amazing Alaska, pages 58-59

1. **d**
2. **False.** There are caribou, salmon, and sand dunes, but no camels.
3. **d**
4. **b**
5. **True.** The icefield is left over from the vast ice sheet that covered much of southern Alaska 23,000 years ago.
6. **d**
7. **c**
8. **Wrangell-St. Elias: F**
9. **Kobuk Valley: A**
10. **Glacier Bay: G**
11. **Katmai: C**
12. **Kenai Fjords: E**
13. **Lake Clark: D**
14. **Denali: B**

The Everglades, pages 62-63

1. **a**
2. **a**
3. **c**
4. **c**
5. **a**
6. **c**
7. **False.** Both alligators and crocodiles have supersensitive dots on their bodies that help them sense pressure and motion. But while a crocodile has about 9,000 of these spots all over its body, an alligator has just about 4,000 of them, concentrated around its face and jaw.
8. **a**
9. **d**
10. **c**
11. **b**
12. **a**
13. **False.** The Everglades receives little to no rainfall from December to April.

Name That Rock, page 65

A. **granite**
B. **sandstone**
C. **olivine**
D. **shale**

Dive In, page 66

What in the World? page 67

From top left, across rows:
RAIN FOREST, VOLCANO, SEA TURTLE
WATERFALL, MONK SEAL, PEARL HARBOR
COQUI FROG, KOA TREE, OHI'A LEHUA

Trading Places, pages 70-71

1. **sea star**
2. **black bear**
3. **chuckwalla**
4. **happy face spider**
5. **golden eagle**

Dive and Discover, pages 72-73

Name That Track, page 74
A. **mountain lion**
B. **black bear**
C. **crow**
D. **raccoon**

What in the World? page 76
From top left, across rows:
BUTTERFLY, GOLDENROD, RED SALAMANDER
MOUNTAIN LAUREL, RED FOX, BLUE JAY
VIRGINIA CREEPER, BOBCAT, RACCOON

Map Mania! Battlefields, pages 78-79
1. **b**
2. **a**
3. **a**
4. **c**
5. **c**
6. **d**
7. **False.** The Nez Perce were seeking to escape from U.S. soldiers by crossing the border into Canada.
8. **Fort Sumter, South Carolina: G**
9. **Little Bighorn, Montana: C**
10. **Boston, Massachusetts: D**
11. **Fort McHenry, Maryland: F**
12. **Gettysburg, Pennsylvania: E**
13. **San Juan, Puerto Rico: A**
14. **Big Hole, Montana: B**

Take a Look! Acadia National Park, page 80

Stump Your Parents, page 82
1. **True.** Photographer Ansel Adams became famous for his striking black-and-white photographs of Yosemite, starting in the 1920s.
2. **d**
3. **c**
4. **c**
5. **b**
6. **a**
7. **b**
8. **False.** In 1947, Hopi artist Fred Kabotie painted murals featuring scenes of traditional Hopi life and cultural symbols at the Painted Desert Inn, in Petrified Forest National Park, Arizona.
9. **d**

Name That Leaf, page 84

A. **sugar maple**
B. **quaking aspen** (also called other names including trembling aspen, white poplar, popple, and quakies)
C. **poison oak**
D. **American holly**

Grand Teton Adventure, page 85

Find the Hidden Animals, page 86

1. **D**
2. **E**
3. **C**
4. **B**
5. **A**

What in the World? page 88

From top left, across rows:
TENT, SLEEPING BAG, COMPASS
SWISS ARMY PENKNIFE, BACKPACK, CAMPFIRE
FRYING PAN, BINOCULARS, FLASHLIGHT

A Distinct Desert, pages 90-91

1. **a**
2. **True.** The venom of a desert rattlesnake is very potent and requires about 20 vials of antivenom, a medicine made from the venom of the snake.
3. **c**
4. **False.** These creatures release a very strong, unpleasant scent.
5. **a**   8. **b**
6. **c**   9. **c**
7. **b**
10. **False.** Only about 500 kinds of plants in the Sonoran Desert are edible.
11. **c**
12. **True.** It can get this hot in the area near the tip of Mexico.
13. **c**
14. **b**

Double Take, Mount Rushmore, page 92

Name That Beach Animal, page 94

A. **glossy ibis**
B. **loggerhead turtle**
C. **wild horses**
D. **horseshoe crab**

Stump Your Parents, page 95

1. **b**
2. **d**
3. **b**
4. **True.** Golden eagles have been known to attack animals as large as deer, mountain goats, and wolves.
5. **c**
6. **c**
7. **b**
8. **True.** If a bald eagle catches a heavy fish, rather than trying to lift it out of the water, it may swim its dinner ashore, using its wings to paddle.
9. **b**

Grand Getaway, pages 96-97

BONUS SCIENCE GAME: Things that are moving include the toy helicopter, the Frisbee, and the bald eagle. Things that are storing energy include the golden retriever and the football.

Name That Feather, page 100

A. **wild turkey**
B. **blue jay**
C. **barred owl**
D. **red flicker**

Beachcomber's Bonanza, pages 104-105

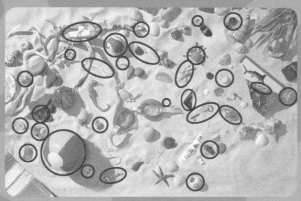

Stump Your Parents, page 106

1. **a**
2. **d**
3. **True.** Scientists have reached this conclusion (which is an estimate) based on evidence including fossils of extinct organisms from trilobites to dinosaurs.
4. **d**
5. **a**
6. **b**
7. **True.** A small group of wolves migrated across an ice bridge on the lake in the 1940s, but over time their lack of genetic diversity has caused their numbers to decline.
8. **c**
9. **b**

Cool Caves, pages 108-109

1. **d**
2. **b**
3. **a**
4. **False.** Bats sleep and live in many different places in addition to caves, including forests, cliffs, and buildings.
5. **d**
6. **a**
7. **a**
8. **a**
9. **a**
10. **b**
11. **d**
12. **a**
13. **b**
14. **d**

Presidential Parks Trivia Challenge, pages 110-111

1. **D**
2. **C**
3. **D**
4. **C**
5. **D**
6. **B**
7. **C**
8. **A**

Name That Amphibian, page 113

A. **red-spotted toad**
B. **spotted salamander**
C. **northern Pacific tree frog**
D. **California red-legged frog**

What in the World? page 115

From top left, across rows:
SPRING PEEPER FROG, QUEEN OF THE NIGHT, MILKY WAY
LIGHTHOUSE, LITTLE BROWN BAT, FIREFLY
FULL MOON, AURORA BOREALIS, HAWK MOTH

Redwood Roundup, page 117

Map Mania! Historic Trails, pages 118-119

1. **a**
2. **b**
3. **a**
4. **c**
5. **b**
6. **a**
7. **c**
8. **Pony Express: B**, red trail
9. **Selma-Montgomery: F**
10. **Lewis and Clark: A**, light green trail
11. **Iditarod: G**, dark green trail
12. **Captain John Smith: E**, orange area
13. **Mormon Pioneers: C**, orange trail
14. **Trail of Tears: D**, yellow trails

Name That Campsite Critter, page 120

A. **raccoon**
B. **garter snake**
C. **ground squirrel**
D. **eastern fence lizard**

Undersea Stars, page 122

Stump Your Parents, page 123

1. **c**
2. **a**
3. **b**
4. **d**
5. **d**
6. **d**
7. **a**
8. **d**

Watery Wonders, pages 124-125

1. **a.**
2. **c.**
3. **b.**
4. **d**
5. **c**
6. **b**
7. **d**
8. **a**
9. **c**
10. **b**
11. **a.**

National Mall, Washington, D.C., pages 128-129

1. **c**
2. **d**
3. **a**
4. **a**
5. **c**
6. **False.** He made his speech on the steps of the Lincoln Memorial.
7. **d**
8. **b**
9. **b**
10. **c**
11. **d**

The River Wild, page 130

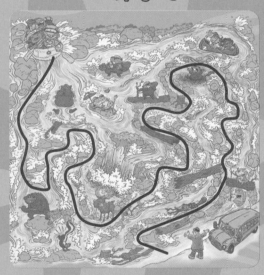

What in the World?, page 131

From top left, across rows:
CLIFF DWELLING, PETROGLYPH, DREAM CATCHER
CANOE, POTTERY, MOCCASIN
JEWELRY, PUEBLO, ARROWHEAD

Take a Look! Yellowstone National Park, page 133

Stump Your Parents, page 134

1. **d**
2. **a**
3. **d**
4. **b**
5. **c**
6. **True.** Lafitte roamed the Louisiana swamps and aided the United States in the War of 1812.
7. **a**
8. **b**
9. **c**

Find the Hidden Animals, page 135

1. **A**
2. **D**
3. **C**
4. **B**

What in the World? page 138

From top left, across rows:
BADGER, EAGLE, SALAMANDER
ROADRUNNER, SNOWSHOE HARE, RACCOON
FLY, LOBSTER, MOUNTAIN GOAT

National Parks Trivia Challenge, pages 140-141

1. **B**
2. **C**
3. **D**
4. **D**
5. **C**
6. **A**
7. **False.** The National Museum of American History holds some of Bell's early telephones, and a special exhibit there allows visitors to hear experimental sound recordings Bell made.

Dog Daze, page 142

Map Mania! Extreme Parks, pages 144 -145

1. **c**
2. **a**
3. **a**
4. **b**
5. **c**
6. **b**
7. **a**
8. **Great Basin: D**
9. **Death Valley: C**
10. **Hot Springs: E**
11. **Congaree: G**
12. **Crater Lake: A**
13. **Mammoth Cave: F**
14. **Acadia: B**

Photo and Illustration credits

Park Index

Page numbers in bold indicate a national park.

ALABAMA
Selma to Montgomery National Historic Trail, 118
Trail of Tears National Historic Trail, 119

ALASKA
Denali National Park and Preserve, **11, 16, 47, 59**
Gates of the Arctic National Park and Preserve, **41**
Glacier Bay National Park and Preserve, **10, 58**
Iditarod National Historic Trail, 119
Katmai National Park and Preserve, **58**
Kenai Fjords National Park, **59, 114, 125**
Kobuk Valley National Park, **58, 75**
Lake Clark National Park and Preserve, **59**
Sitka National Historical Park, 134
Wrangell-St. Elias National Park and Preserve, **58**

AMERICAN SAMOA
National Park of American Samoa, **89, 124**

ARIZONA
Grand Canyon National Park, **30–31, 34, 65, 71, 96–97, 120, 143**
Lake Mead National Recreation Area, 121
Petrified Forest National Park, **77, 82, 151**
Saguaro National Park, **82, 90**
Sunset Crater Volcano National Monument, 112

ARKANSAS
Hot Springs National Park, **144**
Trail of Tears National Historic Trail, 119

CALIFORNIA
Cabrillo National Monument, 134
Channel Islands National Park, **106, 125**
Death Valley National Park, **20, 25, 38, 61, 71, 98, 100, 144**
Golden Gate National Recreation Area, 22, 36, 121
Joshua Tree National Park, **24, 90**
Kings Canyon National Park, **82**
Lassen Volcanic National Park, **112**
Lava Beds National Monument, 103
Pinnacles National Park, **46, 95, 113**
Point Reyes National Seashore, 94, 99, 104
Pony Express National Historic Trail, 118
Redwood National Park, **21, 61, 77, 117**
Rosie the Riveter/World War II Home Front National Historical Park, 123
Santa Monica Mountains National Recreation Area, 121
Sequoia National Park, **11**
Yosemite National Park, **65, 69, 70, 75, 82, 121, 127**

COLORADO
Black Canyon of the Gunnison National Park, **21, 42**
Great Sand Dunes National Park and Preserve, **57, 87**
Mesa Verde National Park, **11**
Pony Express National Historic Trail, 118

Rocky Mountain National Park, **55, 87, 95, 116, 124**

DELAWARE
Captain John Smith Chesapeake National Historic Trail, 119

FLORIDA
Biscayne National Park, **27, 29, 48, 89, 94, 106, 122**
Dry Tortugas National Park, **72**
Everglades National Park, **25, 62–63, 93, 107**

GEORGIA
Trail of Tears National Historic Trail, 119

HAWAII
Haleakalā National Park, **20, 67**
Hawai'i Volcanoes National Park, **24, 67, 83, 121, 136**

IDAHO
Lewis and Clark National Historic Trail, 118
Yellowstone National Park, **10, 13, 74, 75, 82, 106, 110, 121, 123, 133**

ILLINOIS
Lewis and Clark National Historic Trail, 118
Mormon Pioneer National Historic Trail, 119
Trail of Tears National Historic Trail, 119

IOWA
Lewis and Clark National Historic Trail, 118
Mormon Pioneer National Historic Trail, 119

KANSAS
Lewis and Clark National Historic Trail, 118
Pony Express National Historic Trail, 118

KENTUCKY
Mammoth Cave National Park, **108, 145**
Trail of Tears National Historic Trail, 119

LOUISIANA
Jean Lafitte National Historical Park and Preserve, 134

MAINE
Acadia National Park, **27, 40, 43, 80, 101, 103, 121, 125, 145**

MARYLAND
Assateague Island National Seashore, 94
Captain John Smith Chesapeake National Historic Trail, 119
Clara Barton National Historic Site, 123

MASSACHUSETTS
Adams National Historical Park, 110
Lowell National Historical Park, 141
Minute Man National Historical Park, 82

MICHIGAN
Isle Royale National Park, **106, 125**
Keweenaw National Historical Park, 141
Pictured Rocks National Lakeshore, 103

MINNESOTA
Voyageurs National Park, **11**

MISSOURI
Lewis and Clark National Historic Trail, 118
Pony Express National Historic Trail, 118
Trail of Tears National Historic Trail, 119

MONTANA
Glacier National Park, **10, 20, 55, 103**
Lewis and Clark National Historic Trail, 118
Yellowstone National Park, **10, 13, 74, 75, 82, 106, 110, 121, 123, 133**

NEBRASKA
Lewis and Clark National Historic Trail, 118
Mormon Pioneer National Historic Trail, 119
Pony Express National Historic Trail, 118

NEVADA
Death Valley National Park, **20, 25, 38, 61, 71, 98, 100, 144**
Great Basin National Park, **77, 144**
Lake Mead National Recreation Area, 121
Pony Express National Historic Trail, 118

NEW JERSEY
Gateway National Recreation Area, 121
Thomas Edison National Historical Park, 140

NEW MEXICO
Carlsbad Caverns National Park, **11, 25, 26, 108–109**

NEW YORK
Eleanor Roosevelt National Historic Site, 123
Gateway National Recreation Area, 121

NORTH CAROLINA
Great Smoky Mountains National Park, **10, 71, 98, 49, 57, 113, 121**
Trail of Tears National Historic Trail, 119
Wright Brothers National Memorial, 141

NORTH DAKOTA
Lewis and Clark National Historic Trail, 118
Theodore Roosevelt National Park, **11**

OHIO
Cuyahoga Valley National Park, **103, 121**

OKLAHOMA
Trail of Tears National Historic Trail, 119

OREGON
Crater Lake National Park, **112, 145**
Lewis and Clark National Historic Trail, 118
Lewis and Clark National Historical Park, 123

PENNSYLVANIA
Benjamin Franklin National Memorial, 140
Steamtown National Historic Site, 140

SOUTH CAROLINA
Congaree National Park, **19, 124, 144**

SOUTH DAKOTA
Badlands National Park, 10
Lewis and Clark National Historic Trail, 118
Mount Rushmore National Memorial, 46, 50–51, 92, 99
Wind Cave National Park, 41, 106, 108

TENNESSEE
Great Smoky Mountains National Park, 10, 40, 49, 57, 113, 121
Trail of Tears National Historic Trail, 119

TEXAS
Big Bend National Park, 44, 130
Guadalupe Mountains National Park, 21, 46
Padre Island National Seashore, 29, 56

U.S. VIRGIN ISLANDS
Christiansted National Historic Site, 134
Virgin Islands National Park, 25, 27, 70, 73

UTAH
Arches National Park, 61, 65
Bryce Canyon National Park, 25, 42, 74, 103
Canyonlands National Park, 65
Capitol Reef National Park, 21
Dinosaur National Monument, 32
Golden Spike National Historic Site, 134
Mormon Pioneer National Historic Trail, 119
Pony Express National Historic Trail, 118
Zion National Park, 2–3, 40

VIRGINIA
Assateague Island National Seashore, 94
Captain John Smith Chesapeake National Historic Trail, 119
Maggie L. Walker National Historic Site, 123
Shenandoah National Park, 20, 76, 120
Wolf Trap National Park for the Performing Arts, 82

WASHINGTON
Lewis and Clark National Historic Trail, 118
Mount Rainier National Park, 21, 65
North Cascades National Park, 55
Olympic National Park, 33, 60, 74, 111, 121, 124
San Juan Island National Historical Park, 134

WASHINGTON, D.C.
Captain John Smith Chesapeake National Historic Trail, 119
National Mall, 52, 128–129
Rock Creek Park, 121, 142

WEST VIRGINIA
New River Gorge National River, 121

WISCONSIN
Apostle Islands National Seashore, 103

WYOMING
Grand Teton National Park, 25, 40, 85, 103
Mormon Pioneer National Historic Trail, 119
Pony Express National Historic Trail, 118
Yellowstone National Park, 10, 13, 74, 75, 82, 106, 110, 121, 123, 133

Since 1888, the National Geographic Society has funded more than 12,000 research, exploration, and preservation projects around the world. The Society receives funds from National Geographic Partners, LLC, funded in part by your purchase. A portion of the proceeds from this book supports this vital work.

For more information, please visit nationalgeographic .com, call 1-800-647-5463, or write to the following address:
National Geographic Partners
1145 17th Street N.W.
Washington, D.C. 20036-4688 U.S.A.

Visit us online at nationalgeographic.com/books

For librarians and teachers: ngchildrensbooks.org

More for kids from National Geographic: natgeokids.com

For information about special discounts for bulk purchases, please contact National Geographic Books Special Sales: specialsales@natgeo.com

For rights or permissions inquiries, please contact National Geographic Books Subsidiary Rights: bookrights@natgeo.com

Editorial and Design by Bender Richardson White
Art Direction by Julide Dengel

Trade ISBN: 978-1-4263-2304-1

Printed in China
18/RRDS/2

Be an ULTIMATE EXPLORER!

Discover the wonders of nature underground and in the air.

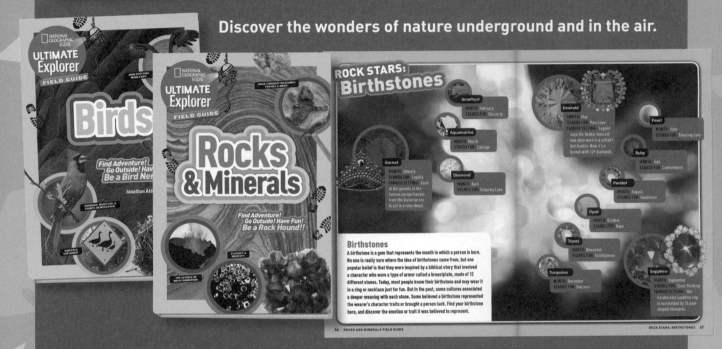

America's NATIONAL PARKS are a great place to practice your outdoor skills.